EXPLORE NEW ZEALAND NATURE

To Keith Lees
He tohu iti o te whakamihi

EXPLORE NEW ZEALAND
NATURE

Brian Parkinson

WHITE CLOUD BOOKS

Published in 2022 by White Cloud, an imprint of Upstart Press Ltd, Auckland

www.upstartpress.co.nz

26 Greenpark Road, Penrose, Auckland, New Zealand

Copyright © 2022 Upstart Press Ltd
Copyright © 2022 in text: Brian Parkinson
Copyright © 2022 in images: Shutterstock

All rights reserved. No part of this publication may be reproduced, stored in a retrieval system or transmitted, in any form or by any means, electronic, mechanical, photocopying, recording or otherwise, without the prior written permission of the publishers and copyright holders.

ISBN 9781990003639

Project Editor: Duncan Perkinson
Designer: Andrew Davies
Printed in China

10 9 8 7 6 5 4 3 2 1

Introduction

For millions of years New Zealand sat alone in the vastness of the South Pacific, a unique world where changes, when they did occur, did so at a glacial pace. Then humans arrived on the scene with all the grace and charm of a cyclone.

First came Maori, who in a few short centuries deforested great parts of both islands and with the aid of the kiore and kuri harassed, harried and hunted a greater part of the kararehe whenua, the original fauna, into extinction.

The arrival of Pakeha exponentially worsened the situation. Starting with Cook, early explorers, sealers, whalers and settlers accidentally introduced vermin whose effects on the native fauna were catastrophic. Cook and other early visitors, such as de Surville, also deliberately introduced foreign animals, always with good intentions but seldom with comparable results.

Since then, all too often the attitude towards our environment has been an unhappy compromise between those who thought the resources were inexhaustible, or who just didn't care, and those who thought the opposite and were determined to get 'theirs' while they could. Perhaps most shameful were the bird collectors – people like Walter Buller and Andreas Reischek – who collected thousands of birds and drove some species to the point of extinction.

From their writings it is apparent that these gentlemen were convinced that many birds were doomed to extinction, but it also seems that they devoted entirely too much of their energies to bringing this state about. It is often argued that the collectors were 'children of the time' and that their actions were typical of the Victorian era. This argument is, however, facile: both Thomas Potts and Richard Henry were contemporaries of Buller and Reischek and both had a much more compassionate understanding and feeling for the land and its creatures.

In my wanderings over the past 75 or so years throughout New Zealand I have noted the dramatic and often draconian changes that are still altering our landscape, an acceleration of the cultural component of our natural history. After all, natural history is as much about history as it is about nature.

This history takes many forms and comes to us in many ways: from the sayings, legends and place names of the tangata whenua, by way of the often florid but always readable accounts of the early naturalists and explorers, and so on to the commentaries of today's observers – more dispassionate but no less caring than their predecessors.

And finally, there is the eloquent testimony of the remnant populations of today's forests and offshore islands – stark legacy of the last 1,000 years of human history. Travelling to such places as the Huiarau Range, Kakapo Bay, Piopiotahi and Papamoa brings a pang of nostalgia for those hapless creatures immortalised in name, but now vanished forever.

And yet a sense of perspective is needed. The changes are constant and continuing and were not started, but rather accelerated, by the arrival of humans on our shores.

So it is interesting to contemplate what New Zealand was like when both James Cook first stepped ashore and when Kupe first beached his canoe.

CHAPTER 1

Northland/Te Tai Tokerau

The long narrow peninsula extending nearly 400km north of Auckland is known as Northland or Te Tai Tokerau – or occasionally, in flights of fancy, as the 'winterless north'.

The east and west coast of the peninsula differ dramatically. In the east there are dozens of superb sandy beaches and excellent harbours which once provided stages for the coastal shipping which served the north. By contrast, the west coast extends in a long curve from Cape Reinga to Auckland, broken only by the Kaipara and Hokianga harbours. This is sometimes called 'the Kauri Coast.'

Geologically, Northland has a varied history. Ancient volcanic plugs, such as those of St Peter and St Paul at Whangaroa and Mt Manaia at Whangarei, contrast with vast sedimentary deposits and the extensive dunelands backing onto the western beaches. Although nowhere do the mountains reach any great heights, the land is rugged and there are few plains except those edging rivers. This factor, along with often poor soil, delayed development of the north until relatively recently.

When Pakeha arrived Northland was covered with forest, dominated by kauri, a tree of great size and with excellent timber. The logging and milling of kauri was the principal industry north of Auckland for many years after Pakeha settlement and, although there are a few stands left, the great trees that once flourished in this area are now mostly gone. Today, the small patches of native bush that remain between Auckland and Whangarei are usually too small to support many native birds and the larger stands have few tall trees.

From Kaiwaka, 23 km north of Wellsford, an alternative route north heads out to the coast at Mangawhai. This scenic route rejoins SH1 at Waipu. A few kilometres south of Waipu and just before the road swings inland away from the coast, take Johnson Point Road to the Waipu Estuary. NZ dotterels and variable oystercatchers breed here along with a range of other shorebirds, including the rare fairy tern.

If you stay on SH1, on your right just north of Kaiwaka is Pukekaroro, its symmetrical 300 m cone clothed with young kauri forest, and just north of Pukekaroro is the bare, fluted dome of Bald Rock. SH1 climbs steeply up the southern side of the Brynderwyn Hills, from the top of which there is an expansive view towards the craggy volcanic peaks of the Whangarei Heads, the sweep of Bream Bay and the Hen and Chicken Islands. It was on the largest island Hen/Taranga, that the North Island saddleback (tieke) survived after being exterminated by introduced predators across the rest of the North Island – a classic example of a predator-free island being the salvation of a species. Starting in 1964, tieke were successfully transferred by the Wildlife Service from Taranga, first to Middle Chicken, then to Red Mercury, Cuvier and Big Chicken. Tieke flourished on Cuvier and it then became a major source of birds for subsequent translocations. These included Kawhitihu, Hauturu, Tiritiri Matangi and Kapiti. Some of these islands in turn became sources for ongoing transfers to various other islands and pest-free mainland sites including Zealandia Eco-sanctuary in Wellington, and Tawharanui. Two species have been translocated to Taranga from other islands – the little spotted kiwi (kiwi pukupuku) from Kapiti and the stitchbird (hihi) from Little Barrier. The kiwi have thrived but the hihi translocation seems to have failed.

From 2013 brown kiwi were reintroduced to Marunui a privately-owned QEII covenant in the Brynderwyns. Kereru, morepork, fernbird, tomtit, fantail, grey warbler, silvereye and tui also occur there along with one of the northernmost populations of Hochstetter's frogs. Shining and long-tailed cuckoo visit seasonally and kaka and bellbird are frequent visitors. On summer evenings both here and further south through the Rodney District, you can often hear the kek-kek-kek calls of Cook's petrels (titi) passing overhead as they return to their burrows on Hauturu, taking a shortcut home across lower Northland from feeding grounds in the Tasman Sea. When Maori arrived, these and other petrels nested on many inland mountain ranges and were an important food source, particularly after they had wiped out the big, meaty moas and other flightless ground birds along with seals and sea lions. Now, almost all the enormous inland petrel colonies have gone, with only a few still nesting in isolated mainland areas such as the Kaikoura Ranges and on the West Coast of the South Island.

About 30 km south of Whangarei, turn right off SH1 and check the Ruakaka Wildlife Reserve. NZ dotterels and variable oystercatchers breed here and a range of other shorebirds also occur here including pied oystercatchers, bar-tailed godwits and lesser knots, of which the last two species are summer visitors. Ruakaka was a former fairy tern breeding site, but as with many other popular east coast beaches, these days breeding shorebirds have to contend with beachgoers and their dogs, especially during the busy summer season. Many shorebird breeding sites are now managed by local community groups, who fence off dotterel nesting territories and help to enforce seasonal dog bans. This work has resulted in a remarkable recovery of the NZ dotterel population, and dotterels have been expanding their range to southern North Island sites where they last bred over a century ago. If you carry on beyond Ruakaka, you reach the mouth of the Whangarei Harbour at Marsden Point, the site of New Zealand's only oil refinery. Here you can mix views of industry with the spectacular backdrop of Mt Manaia, just across the harbour.

The kaka that gave Ruakaka its name are now only occasional visitors, and such commemorative names serve as a sad reminder of the natural paradise of old New Zealand. Others such as Waikereru (water of the kereru), Waiparera (water of the grey duck) and Mangatete (river of the grey teal) are just a few of the very many such place names dotted about the north.

It is not far from here, at Tangiteroria, that Walter Buller, perhaps the best known of New Zealand's early ornithologists, spent his youth and developed his passion for collecting. Near his father's mission station he collected what he believed to be the last piopio in the north and later penned what must surely be one of the most extraordinary and odious contributions ever made to our ornithological literature in which he recalled:

...the bright dewy morning, now five-and-thirty years ago, when I shot

my first kohoperoa [long-tailed cuckoo] *in the old Mission-garden at Tangiteroria, and found my beautiful prize lying on the sward with its banded wings and tail stretched out to their full extent. I have remembered the delight with which, almost as long ago, I shot in the Tangihua mountains my first piopio, a bird so rare in the far north, even at that time, that it was entirely unknown to the natives of the district.*

It is very easy to see why people such as Buller, Reischek and other collectors were detested by early conservationists such as Richard Henry and Thomas Potts.

In Whangarei, a visit to the information centre on SH1, will provide directions to the many parks and walks in the area. And if you have the time, a 35 km drive south-east of the city to Ocean Beach will enable you to see many seabirds and study the strange, craggy volcanic peaks at the Whangarei Heads.

From Whangarei north to the Bay of Islands the scenery is constantly changing, from farmland to swamp to scrub and then to forest, and this wide and often abrupt variation means a corresponding variation in the life living there. If you are interested in seabirds, take a detour from Whangarei to Ngunguru, Tutukaka, Matapouri and Whananaki, returning to the main route at Whakapara, 22 km north of Whangarei.

Tutukaka is now a site of great interest to birders, particularly those whose penchant is seabirds. There are a number of trips out of Tutukaka, which offer the chance to see seabirds but these are generally just an add-on to trips to the Poor Knights Islands for scuba diving or for dolphin and whale watching. You will be better served by taking a bespoke pelagic seabird spotting tour such as that offered by Tutukaka 'Petrel Station' Pelagics. The lists of birds from their trips are very impressive. In addition to many of the common tubenoses such as Buller's and flesh-footed shearwaters, summer trip lists have included black and Pycroft's petrels, New Zealand and white-faced storm petrels, grey ternlets and even white-naped petrels, which are rare visitors from the Kermadec Islands.

From Whangarei there are two routes north: one is the coast road via Oakura, which provides wonderful coastal scenery and passes Whangaruru

Harbour, home to many seabirds and waders. The other is SH1 and from Whakapara north to Kawakawa you will see mainly exotic birds, such as thrushes, blackbirds and flocks of finches, with kingfishers relatively plentiful along the waterways.

Kawakawa, 54 km north-west of Whangarei, is named for the pepper tree, which is relatively common in areas of secondary growth, but there are none in Kawakawa itself. One wonders why the district council doesn't plant a few. However I am told that there is one growing on the roof of the Hundertwasser designed public toilets.

Although Russell is only a short distance from Kawakawa by way of the Opua car ferry, take the back road through Taumarere where there are extensive areas of scrub and swamp. You might even be lucky enough to see a fernbird in marshy areas abutting the road, although its habitat has been greatly reduced.

Besides the large areas of gorse, blackberry flourish and small clumps of once carefully nurtured exotic trees, as well as lilies and yellow irises. The ubiquitous macrocarpa are yet another reminder of the economic decline of the north, marking as they do the sites of former homesteads. There are some patches of kauri forest that escaped the logger's axe and there are still a few kiwi along with tui and kereru.

The kereru is sometimes called kukupa in the north.

Once called Kororareka, Russell was a major supply port for the many whalers operating in the Pacific in the early part of the 19th century. Working from here they relentlessly pursued pods of right whales along the coast. Russell is now a centre for big game fishing and the waters off Cape Brett are home to marlin, mako sharks, shoals of trevally and other pelagic fish.

At Whangamumu, not far from Russell, H. H. Cook established a shore-based whaling station and was the first to mechanise the business by using steam-operated chasers in 1910. He also had an innovative way of trapping Humpback whales (paikea) by driving them through a narrow channel where they became entangled in huge steel nets and were thus easier to harpoon.

Whangamumu can be reached from the Oakura road or by driving along the Rawhiti road from Russell. To reach the site of the whaling station, follow a signposted track over the hill to the harbour.

Around Whangamumu there are old tri-pots, slipways and other mementos of its whaling heyday, but the scenery is charming and flocks of gannets can be seen diving just offshore.

The relentless pressure put on whales, and particularly on such vulnerable species as the right whale (waiti wera), brought a number of species close to extinction. Blue whales and sperm whales are both increasing, with growing numbers of blue whales now being seen off the Taranaki coast.

While in this area drive to Oke Bay, favoured by dolphins which can sometimes be seen close to the shore. This area is also noteworthy for the early scientific work carried out here. While the *Endeavour* was in the Bay of Islands in December 1769, Joseph Banks collected goatfish, hapuku, blue cod and sea perch here. By coincidence, the *St Jean Baptiste*, commanded by Jean-Francois Marie de Surville, was in the same area only a few days later and they also collected specimens, probably tui, pukeko, kokako, kereru as well as some lizards and the native dog, kuri. Apparently the French appreciated the material collected as much for its culinary qualities as for its scientific value. The French presented a pair of pigs and a hen and chickens to local Maori.

It was not until early in the 19th century that Pakeha exploration in the north really began. One luminary who visited the Bay of Islands was Charles Darwin. Arriving in December 1835 from Tahiti, Darwin was decidedly unimpressed with the inhabitants of the Bay of Islands, despite the settlers' tendency to turn New Zealand into as close an approximation of Britain as possible:

> *At Paihia, it was quite pleasing to behold the English flowers in the gardens before the houses; there were roses of several kinds, honeysuckle, jasmine, stocks, and whole hedges of sweet briar.*

Mention must be made of Northland's most exciting conservation development of recent years, the Project Island Birdsong.

In 2009 a group of local residents started a major drive to clear seven islands in the Bay of Islands of predators and weeds. These are Motuarohia, Motukiekie, Moturua, Okahu, Poroporo, Urupukapuka and Waewaetorea and when they were deemed pest free, five bird species were introduced – tieke, North Island robin (toutouwai), pateke, kakariki and whitehead (popokatea), along with Duvaucel's geckos and wetapunga, and other introductions are planned.

Three of the islands can be reached by ferries from Paihia and Russell but if your time is limited it might pay to concentrate on Urupukupuka, which has a good wharf and nice cafe. On my recent visit a wander through some of the revegetated areas turned up plenty of tieke, piwakawaka and riroriro but the banded rail (moho pereru) near the wharf was probably the twitch of the day. The return trip to Paihia had the bonus of a large pod of dolphins which stayed with us for about 20 minutes.

From Paihia it is an easy drive of less than an hour to the Puketi Forest. The most direct route is from Kerikeri via either the Puketotara or the Pungaere Road. Access to Puketi is well sign-posted and in autumn, along the way, you can see glorious hedgerows or groups of deciduous trees which in recent decades have really blossomed in the north. Chief among these are maples but there are aspens, hickorys, spruces and birches along with trees such as gingkos and tupelo. Best if you ask one of the local tree aficionados for the location of the best specimens.

This kauri forest has been partially logged but one of the most magnificent trees in the north, "Te Tangi o te Tui" (the Lament of the Tui), is found here. This beautiful name was given to the tree by hunters of the Rahiri tribe who were hunting kereru. The forest, besides kauri, also has manuka and kanuka growing on the logged land where the forest is slowly regenerating with good examples of matai, Hall's totara and northern rata, rimu and miro. The lower and more swampy areas are dominated by kahikatea and maire-tawake, the swamp maire. Puketi seems so far to have escaped the worst ravages of the Kauri dieback.

The birds here include robins, kaka, kakariki, kereru and tui as well as grey warblers, fantails, pied tits and silvereyes and at night kiwi and morepork are often heard.

Puketi is also home to one of the rarest of our bush birds, the kokako, and thanks to a valiant effort it is starting to make a comeback. At the last count at the end of 2020, there were 15 birds with 6 pairs.

Although the kokako is not particularly secretive, the best way to locate one is by listening for its distinctive flute-like calls which vary from area to area. I once wondered how kokako, transferred to Little Barrier from various parts of the North Island, surmounted these language difficulties, but it seems they didn't. It took a couple of visits to Puketi before I found that the best time to listen for these songs is just after dawn. Accordingly, one rather foggy, wintry morning a few years ago, Keith Lees, a friend from Kawakawa and I visited Puketi. It took about an hour along a very wet and slippery trail for us to get into a good position on a ridge top where we could clearly hear the birds. We had only just settled into position when a pair of paradise shelduck flew over and spent the next half hour circling us squawking. Needless to say, by the time they had finished every other bird had long since decamped and for the only time in my life I sympathised with duck shooters.

From Puketi it is an easy run north to Kaeo where brown teals still survive in what is the largest colony of these ducks outside Great Barrier/ Aotea Island. You can get there most directly from Puketi by taking the unsealed road through Waiare and this joins SH10 just south of Kaeo. From Kaeo north on this road the coast has mostly gulls and terns together with shags and NZ dotterels, but the road runs through gumland scrub so land birds are few. Both Doubtless Bay and Rangaunu Bay have Caspian and white-fronted terns, oystercatchers, wrybills, godwits, turnstones and knots but these are usually pretty wary and difficult to see if you don't have a boat. The mangrove creeks around here are occasionally frequented by royal spoonbills, along with the kotuku, or white heron, up from their breeding grounds in the South Island. These are most easily seen when they move out onto the mudflats to feed.

From Kaeo it is about a further 60 km to Awanui, and there a short detour from SH1 will take you to Lake Waiparera on the Aupouri Peninsula. Here there are shags, ducks and black swans together with a few waders. From

Awanui north to Cape Reinga one passes first through scrubland and then, nearer the top of the North Island, rolling farmland, some of which is in grass. A stop at Tangoake Landing near Te Kao, 46 km south-west of Cape Reinga, is worth making as the swamp here is good fernbird and rail habitat. Also, according to some local birders, it is worthwhile looking in local ponds for hoary-headed grebes (taihoropi) and little grebes (tokitokipio) as there are historical records of these being found here.

Parengarenga has a couple of possible translations. One is the pa where the renga, a lily, grew; the other is the pa of the native spinach. It would be nice to think that the harbour was named after this pretty white flower with its centre of lavender and yellow, but it is probably named after the spinach.

North Cape is a refuge for some of our rarest plants. In the serpentine outcrops, which extend only over a few square kilometres, are found more than a dozen local endemics, including some very rare ones. Another rarity of the far north is the pupuharakeke, the flax snail. Predation by pigs and rats has reduced it to a few tiny populations restricted to pockets of bush near Cape Reinga. Measures to help the pupuharakeke include poisoning rats and planting flax and other native trees to increase its habitat. The travelling naturalist should also check out the small bush remnants for ferns as some mainland rarities are found here including the coastal brake, *Pteris comans* and *Todea barbara*.

From Cape Reinga itself there are fine views looking north over the turbulent area where the Tasman Sea and the Pacific Ocean meet. Seabirds frequent the seas around here, but they are usually too far away to be easily seen. Here too, is the sacred pohutukawa from which the spirits of Maori departed for the spirit world. The setting off point is known as Akikite Reinga.

Each year Piwhane/Spirits Bay on Cape Reinga is host to a remarkable event. In March godwits from all parts of the country assemble here for their heroic flight north to their breeding grounds in the Arctic tundra of western Alaska, well over 12,000 km! James Buckland left a vivid picture of this departure, written in the 1890s:

The beach was covered with kuaka ...thousands hovering overhead to find a footing...an old cock uttered a strident call, clarion clear, and shot straight into the air followed by an incalculable feathered multitude. Higher and higher the host rose until it was just a stain in the sky.

It is interesting to contemplate what this area must have been like when Maori first arrived. A midden excavated near here, dating from the 13th century, contained the remains of 77 fur seals and another at Houhora, just to the south, had 44 fur seals, 8 sea lions and 7 sea elephants, indicating the former presence of substantial numbers of these animals along the coast. In other middens further south the remains of yet another species, the sea leopard, have also been found.

From Cape Reinga one can return south either by the road or via Ninety Mile Beach which is best attempted at low tide with a 4WD. Once this coast was a rich source of shellfish like toheroa and tuatua, as well as being a particularly productive fishing ground. Now the toheroa are in such low numbers that their collection is strictly regulated and the fishing has also declined because of overfishing offshore.

After returning to SH1 near Awanui the road takes you through planted pine forests. Not much birdlife is found apart from the usual exotics, but pairs of paradise shelduck can often be seen in the open patches among the trees together with herons and stilts near the occasional ponds.

From Kaitaia the direct route south takes you through the Mangamuka Bush where there are still kiwi and the now rarely seen kakariki. There are also still some kereru but these are now in very low numbers. In the north, they are generally called kukupa.

From here it is not far to the Hokianga Harbour and the most direct route is by way of the rather tortuous road to Rangiora, along the upper reaches of the Hokianga Harbour. From the Narrows, ferries leave regularly during the day for Rawene on the harbour's southern side where you can take SH12 for the 25 km drive to Opononi.

This village was, for one brief summer in 1955-56, home to one of our best-known animals – Opo – a female bottle-nosed dolphin (terehu) who enjoyed the company of swimmers. Opo is now commemorated by a statue in the town centre. Dolphins still occasionally frequent the bay and fur seals frequently haul out in bad weather.

Amateur botanists will find the Waima Forest, not far from Opononi on the Kaikohe road, of interest. Here two plant discoveries were made in the 1980s: an undescribed *Olearia* in 1984 and a new *Coprosma* in 1987.

From the Hokianga the road south takes you to the Waipoua State Forest, home to our two most magnificent trees, the giant kauri 'Tane Mahuta' (Lord of the Forest) and 'Te Matua Ngahere' (Father of the Forest). These trees have been growing in the Waipoua for between 1,200 and 1,500 years and would have been sizeable trees when Maori first arrived. It is a sobering thought that, big as these trees are, bigger specimens once grew in New Zealand. Tane Mahuta has a girth of 13.77 m but the mighty Kairaru Kauri on Mt. Tutamoe, about 25 km south-east, had a girth of 20.1 m and the Trounson Kauri next to the Trounson Kauri Park was also bigger. Both the Trounson Kauri and the Kairaru Kauri were destroyed in enormous forest fires which devastated this area in the late 1880s and the early 1890s. There are signs of kauri dieback in the forest but Tane Mahuta so far seems to be OK and stringent measures to protect it are in force.

From Waipoua, SH12 eventually brings you to the Trounson Kauri Park. Here, there is a nice collection of trees in pleasant surrounds, although after Waipoua the kauri seem a little puny. Because the park is fairly small and is not beside any sizeable area of native bush there are virtually no native birds here. It is a bit unusual to sit in native forest and listen to a chorus of exotic birds such as mynas, magpies, blackbirds and rosellas. However it is possible to see kiwi at night but you need to work this out with the park management.

On the opposite side of SH12 from the Trounson Kauri Park is the Taharoa Domain and the Kai Iwi Lakes – Waikere, Taharoa and Kai Iwi. The lakes provide a home for a number of species of waterbirds, including NZ dabchicks and shags and both the hoary-headed grebe and the little grebe have also been recorded here. Numerous ducks also occur and the numbers of these burgeon in the shooting season. The lakes also provide some of the northernmost trout fishing in New Zealand.

Travelling further south brings you to the Kaipara Harbour, another important assembly and feeding point for wading birds. A giant petrel, sometimes known rather unkindly as the stinkpot, arrived near Dargaville almost 10,500 km from where it was banded in the South Orkneys and other birds such as the red-tailed tropic bird (amokura) have also been found in this area. The amokura was highly prized by Maori for its two long, red, central tail feathers.

Jane Mander in her book *The Story of a New Zealand River*, written in the early part of the 20th century, gives us a delightful account of the riverine scenery of the Kaipara:

> *From the mangrove banks to the sky a great variety of trees in fifty shades of evergreen covered every yard of space. There was a riotous spring colour in the forest, voluptuous gold and red in the clumps of yellow kowhai and crimson rata, and there were masses of greeny white clematis and bowers of pale tree fern to rest the satiated eye. Stiff laurel-like puriris stood beside the dropping fringe of the lacey rimu: hard blackish kahikateas brooded over the oak-like ti-toki with its lovely scarlet berry.*

This, presumably, was before goats, deer and possums arrived.

CHAPTER 2

Auckland/Tamaki Makaurau

Travelling south towards Auckland on SH1, along the 'Hibiscus Coast' the first place of interest is Kawau Island, just off the coast from Warkworth. Last century this was the home of Governor George Grey, who introduced to the island several species of exotic animals, including kookaburras, monkeys, zebra and five species of wallaby. In quite an interesting twist, one of these, the Parma wallaby, survived on Kawau after it disappeared in its homeland, Australia, and some were re-exported there – a popular New Zealand immigrant to Australia. Ferries to Mansion House, the former home of Governor Grey, leave regularly from Sandspit, and once a day a mail run calls into the numerous small bays in Bon Accord Harbour.

Lying on a narrow peninsula just north of Kawau is Auckland Council-administered Tawharanui Regional Park, which you reach via Takatu Road just east of Matakana. Within the park is the 550 ha Tawharanui Open Sanctuary, a 'mainland island' protected by a pest-proof fence completed in 2004. Soon after the fence was built and pest mammals removed, kākā and bellbirds colonised naturally from Hauturu. The bellbird is now one of the most numerous bush birds in the sanctuary, and very easily seen on the tracks through Ecology Bush in the centre of the park. As with Shakespear Open Sanctuary, a number of rare birds have been introduced including brown kiwi, takahe, pateke, red-crowned kakariki, whitehead, robin and tieke. Tawharanui is an excellent place to see kiwi. On summer evenings many kiwi leave the forest and forage in the paddocks near the bush margins. A walk eastwards along the peninsula during the first couple of hours after dusk is well worth it. Listen out also for spotless crakes, which in this pest free environment, occupy both wetland and upland habitats. As you enter the park, pause as you cross the stream that flows into the lagoon, because it is a good place to see banded rails. Along the road to Anchor Bay, keep a sharp look out for takahe, as their road sense is not great. Both Tawharanui and Shakespear Regional Parks are also notable for their big pukeko populations.

The ocean beaches and dunelands at Tawharanui are a stronghold for shore skinks and have breeding variable oystercatchers and NZ dotterels. Fluttering shearwaters, grey-faced and diving petrels are returning to breed around the clifftops at Takatu Point and on summer evenings, listen for the cries of Cook's petrels returning to Hauturu from the Tasman Sea. An active community group, the Tawharanui Open Sanctuary Society (TOSSI), supports conservation work in the park and volunteers are always welcome.

Just north of Tawharanui is Omaha Beach, now very built up with seaside baches. At the northern end of Omaha is a predator-fenced spit, which has breeding populations of variable oystercatchers and NZ dotterels, and also the largest high tide shorebird roost along this stretch of coast. In autumn, Omaha Spit has a large post-breeding flock of over 100 NZ dotterels. Forming a backdrop to Omaha is an impressive kahikatea forest, which grades into an extensive saltmarsh, home to banded rails and fernbirds.

From Omaha turn right onto the road to Leigh. Just beyond Leigh, a short drive leads to Goat Island/Te Hawere-a-Maki Marine Reserve. When this reserve was first proposed by scientists based at the nearby University of Auckland Leigh Marine Laboratory, there was much grumbling from local fishermen, but the marine reserve, established in 1975 and New Zealand's first, soon proved its worth by allowing snapper, crayfish and other species to attain breeding size and repopulate other areas. Snorkelling is very easy and at low tide it is possible to see a great variety of marine life while swimming in shallow water. The fish are unusually tame, and although this is discouraged, are often hand fed. Wear gloves though, as their teeth are sharp, and it's a good idea also to wear a t-shirt.

Goat Island itself has resident colonies of red-billed gulls and white-fronted terns but no longer any goats. Also here are the burrows of a small colony of grey-faced petrels, and pied shags nest in the pohutukawa so don't picnic under the shaggery. As on Tiritiri Matangi Island, the forest is in the process of regenerating after a period as grassland. Pohutukawa, mapou, houpara and mahoe are all emerging and it is expected that eventually Goat Island will be covered with the coastal forest once common in this area.

From Goat Island one looks north to Pakiri Beach and the view takes in coastline stretching from the Whangarei Heads down towards distant Moehau, the high point at the tip of the Coromandel Peninsula. Looking eastwards the view is dominated by Hauturu, its lofty summit often capped with cloud, and beyond, the rugged outline of Great Barrier stretches across the eastern horizon. The rare fairy tern (tara iti) breeds in the dunelands at Pakiri Beach and at Mangawhai, where the estuary and dunes are also home to the largest autumn flocking site for NZ dotterels in the country. Offshore, flocks of shearwaters and gannets follow shoals of fish, appearing to cartwheel along as the leading birds dive and then come up and join the tail of the flock.

From Goat Island, the road back to SH1 at Wellsford via Pakiri and Whangaripo climbs steeply above Leigh before descending on the Pakiri side where it then passes through rolling farmland with pockets of bush dominated by totara. For an interesting alternative route, just inland from Pakiri, take the road north towards Tomarata. Three attractive dune lakes, Slipper, Spectacle and Tomarata, lie behind Te Arai Point. Although waterfowl are rather few, all three lakes have good marginal reed beds which are habitat for bittern, spotless crake and fernbird. Sometimes fairy terns feed over Slipper and Spectacle Lakes.

If you are following the west coast road south to Auckland, take SH16 which follows the southern shore of the Kaipara Harbour south to Helensville and then south again to Auckland. It is not so busy as SH1, so unless you are in a hurry it's probably worth taking this route.

If you have time take the road which runs to the end of the South Head of the Kaipara Harbour. As in many places the dairy farms have now been largely supplanted by deer farms. There are large numbers of red deer but also one or two herds of fallow deer, which provide a welcome change, being to my mind more attractive animals. In winter there are often flocks of cattle egrets among the dairy cows as this has been an egret wintering area for about 50 years. Paradise shelducks are often seen in the fields along with a few masked lapwings and many pukeko. Peafowl (pikao), too, are quite common along the bush edges and can be quite clearly seen from the road.

From the Kaipara Harbour back to Auckland there are not many land birds, but look out for waterfowl in lakes such as Rototuna and Roto Otuauru and for recently liberated red-legged partridges around Helensville. Helensville was originally a timber town, founded during the onslaught on the mighty kauri forests which once covered this region. These forests were a slow growing but quickly exploited resource and once they were gone Helensville stagnated for many years, but is now showing signs of a revival.

South again from Helensville one comes to the orchards and vineyards around Henderson and Kumeu. Dalmatian immigrants who arrived during the heyday of the gum-digging started many of these and from fairly modest beginnings this horticulture now covers a wide area, slowly giving way to the inexorable northward spread of Auckland's suburbia.

Without doubt the most striking physical features of the Tamaki/Auckland area are its volcanoes. On any fine day go to the top of such vantage points around the city as Maungawhau/Mt Eden, Owairaka/Mt Albert and Maungakiekie/One Tree Hill – themselves extinct volcanic cones – and you will enjoy panoramic views of the Auckland landscape dotted with the abundant evidence of prior volcanic activity.

To the layperson cones perhaps most typify volcanic activity, but eruptions also leave other marks on the land. Some of these are the water filled depressions exemplified by Lake Pupuke and Orakei and Kaiahiku/Panmure Basins.

Few of the cones have retained their original unsullied symmetry. Offering ideal strategic defense points, they were enthusiastically reshaped into the terraces, ramparts and pits of defensible pas.

Judging by the enormous quantities of soil that were moved by primitive tools and sheer muscle power, fear of attack must have been an effective motivating force.

Indications are that before the 'Musket Wars' the Auckland area was among the most densely settled and most coveted areas in all Aotearoa due, in no small part, to the fertile soils and equitable climate of the region.

All this fortification was to little avail however, particularly when the northern tribes became the first to obtain muskets, and at the time of the first Pakeha settlement the Tamaki Isthmus, where Auckland is now centred, was largely depopulated.

Captain David Rough, who was among the first to inspect the settlement site, wrote in 1840:

> *I climbed up the cliffs to where Ponsonby now is and beheld a vast expanse of undulating country, mostly covered with fern and manuka scrub; several volcanic hills in sight and, near the shore, valleys and ravines in which many species of native plants were growing, whilst the projecting cliffs and headlands were covered with pohutukawa trees – not a sign of human habitation or cultivation, the nearest village being out of sight.*

The Pakeha colonisation of the Auckland area was thorough and rapid. Attracted by the advantages offered by the two great harbours – the Waitemata and the Manukau – and access to the farmable lands to the south and north, Pakeha settlers came in droves and what little 'good timber' there was soon gave way to the axe and fire.

Consequently, Auckland is today one of the most altered of New Zealand's environments, most of the obvious birds and trees being exotics. However, there are pockets of native timber even within the city limits, for example, the Karaka grove in the Auckland Domain, and good stands of trees in the hills to the south and north.

The earliest exotic still standing is a Woollybutt eucalypt planted by the Rev. James Hamlin at Orua Bay on the Manukau in 1836, but my personal favourites include the Kaffir boom in front of Auckland University, the Holm oak at St Barnabas Church in Mt Eden, the Olive Grove in Cornwall Park, the Chilean Wine Palm and the Small-leaved Fig, with its striking buttress roots, at Monte Cecilia Park, Hillsborough Road, and lastly the beautiful Ginkgo biloba and the Tree of Heaven in Albert Park.

The two most common gulls, the black-backed (karoro) and the red-billed (tarapunga), are natives and have adapted well to city life with its rich pickings for scavengers, but other endemics are not so obvious. Walk through the Domain or Cornwall Park and you will probably see, or at least hear, the occasional tui, grey warbler (riroriro), silvereye (tauhou) and fantail (piwakawaka), but the majority of birds will be a motley lot of adventives, mostly from Britain and Europe along with a couple from Australia.

Elsewhere in the city there are numerous small parks and reserves, more than 4,000, few large enough to support viable populations of native birds, but with fine trees nevertheless. Information about these parks can be obtained from the numerous brochures and maps the Auckland City Council regularly produces.

One reserve that does have large numbers of native birds is Tahuna Torea, a 28 ha sandspit and mangrove lagoon projecting into the Tamaki Estuary. A walkway encircles the entire reserve, which takes about an hour to walk around. However, check the tides since part of the walkway is only accessible at low tide. As to be expected, the most common birds seen here are waterfowl – pukeko, grey duck (parera), mallards (rakiraki), and even black swans (kakianau). Of the wading birds, expect to see pied stilts, godwits and pied oystercatchers – the Maori name of Tahuna Torea means 'the gathering place of the oystercatcher'.

Auckland Zoo at Point Chevalier has a relatively good collection of exotic animals in charming surrounds, but now its real strength is its New Zealand collection and the modern, attractive environment in which it is held. There are good collections of waterfowl, but the highlight is its collection of endemic fauna. Here visitors have an opportunity to see species of birds, lizards and invertebrates that are not exhibited anywhere else and the habitats are world class.

Immediately adjoining the Zoo is Western Springs/Te Wai Orea, which is a popular destination for Aucklanders, particularly on weekends. It is a large park surrounding a big, rather murky pond. This would not seem to be prime habitat for birds, but since the large flock of geese (kuihi) that once dominated the pond, polluting the water and terrorising smaller visitors, have been moved away it is now worth spending time there. NZ Dabchicks (weweia) which are rarer, or certainly more secretive, on ponds and lakes elsewhere, are accustomed to visitors and can often be seen on the smaller ponds. Australian Coots, one of our most recent avian migrants, are here and as stroppy as ever, harassing even much larger birds such as black swans (kakianau). There are good numbers of pukeko, NZ scaup (papango), mallards (rakiraki) and on the lawns a number of pairs of our beautiful paradise shelducks (putangitangi).

While the Auckland Museum has a natural history section, the dioramas in Wellington and Christchurch are better and the birds both there and also in Dunedin are not so obviously stuffed.

For those who wish to spend a day in pleasant bush surrounds, head to the Waitakere Ranges and thence to the West Coast beaches. The southernmost beaches of Piha, Karekare and Whatipu can be reached via Titirangi.

The Waitakeres lie to the west of Auckland City and some 16,000 ha in this area have been set aside as a reserve with c. 250 km of walking tracks. When Pakeha arrived these hills were covered in kauri forest, but 100 years of logging have removed almost all of the big trees and left us with such anomalies as a 'Lone Kauri' Road without a single large kauri. Much of the bush is secondary growth through which kauri are re-emerging with what seems almost painful slowness.

There are still a few good kauri and perhaps the best of these can be seen on the Large Kauri Walk, which is reached off Scenic Drive via Titirangi and Waiatarua. Look for the signpost, four kilometres past Waiatarua when coming from Auckland. It is not far past the Parkinson Lookout which also has some good native trees.

With the advent of the 'Kauri dieback' disease a number of walks have been closed to protect the trees but information for the various walks in the area can be obtained from the park information centre at Arataki, also on Scenic Drive, 5 km past Titirangi and 24 km from downtown Auckland. They provide a wealth of information on the various aspects of the Waitakere region, particularly on the bush.

A good view over the area, which will enable you to see the amount of logging that has been carried out, can be obtained from the top of Mt Donald McLean, reached by driving up a short, steep side road from the Huia-Whatipu road. As might be expected, the majority of the birds in this area are exotics such as blackbirds, rosellas and even very occasionally kookaburras, but there are a few natives such as silvereyes, tui, warblers and the rare kaka.

Considerable pressure is put on these birds by stoats and rats, and also by the less than charming custom of Aucklanders dumping their unwanted cats here on the somewhat specious theory that this is the kindest thing to do. Not so! Used to being mollycoddled, cats go through a period of abject misery before about 90 per cent of them finally succumb to starvation. Those that don't, in a remarkable display of atavism, become some of the most efficient predators of the bush. Lean, mean and decidedly nasty. Anything further from Tiddles would be hard to imagine.

The settlement of Huia is the interesting result of a whopping misidentification of a bird, as this area is several hundred kilometres from the former range of this beautiful species. What was actually seen is now lost in the mists of time, but it most certainly was not a huia.

If you have time continue on to Whatipu, at the end of the road. This is at the north head of the Manukau Harbour and without traffic is a pleasant enough drive. Among the birds to be seen at the large sandy area at the end of the road are white-faced herons, South Island pied oystercatchers and wrybills in winter, banded and New Zealand dotterels, pied stilts and both Caspian and white-fronted terns.

Before returning to Auckland, take a detour to Piha. Piha, to my mind, is a beach that most typifies New Zealand. Massed grey-green pohutukawa interspersed with waving white pennants of toetoe ascend in serried rows to the skyline, and in boisterous weather the sky is charged with that moody, brooding air which is so characteristic of the wild West Coast. The beach is dominated by the huge Lion Rock, which can be climbed for the superb views from the top.

From here, if you are particularly energetic, you can walk along the seafront the 20 or so kilometres to Muriwai, but this route is difficult and, depending on tides, can be dangerous. Take care to check the weather and tides before starting off as the sea around here can sometimes get very rough indeed. You will certainly see gulls and perhaps gannets and there is now a colony of fur seals which haul out on the rocks here in the non-breeding season and there is even a very small chance of seeing a Maui's dolphin (upokehue) offshore.

Muriwai, the next major beach north, requires a detour back through Waimauku if you wish to reach it by road. At the south end of the beach is one of the only three mainland nesting colonies of the Australasian gannet (takapu) – the others being the one established about 40 years ago at Farewell Spit at the north-eastern point of the South Island and the well-known gannetry at Cape Kidnappers in Hawkes Bay. You can get a good view of the domestic tribulations of the gannets from the hill above. They arrive here to nest around the end of September and the young birds, like so many other young New Zealanders, head off to Australia for their formative years. At around two years of age they begin to return to our waters – never to leave again. Gannets are among the few native birds to be on the increase and are vigorously in the process of establishing new colonies.

Muriwai is also noted as one of the 'hotspots' for whale strandings although these are not all that common. The largest stranding of sperm whales to take place in our waters was here in 1974 when 72 animals came ashore. Altogether, since records have been kept, there have been 5 herd and 12 individual strandings of this species at Muriwai and other cetacean species have come ashore not far along the coast.

Another interesting drive to take out of Auckland is south to Miranda on the Firth of Thames. Turn off SH1 at Otara in South Auckland, then travel to the coast again at Kawakawa Bay through Clevedon. On the way you pass through mainly pastoral country with its inevitable introduced birds. Here I saw a red-legged partridge, which is our most recent bird introduction. About 10,000 or so have been released in the Auckland area by the Auckland Acclimatisation Society since 1980. To my mind it is a pleasantly coloured and charming bird and a great improvement on such birds as the house sparrow (tiu), which were first imported by the same society in 1865.

Although it could be considered heretical to say so, most of these bird introductions were not entirely unwelcome, except for perhaps that of that arch-villain, the magpie (makipai). The depredations of both Maori and Pakeha left a very large gap indeed in our fauna and presumably an even larger temptation to fill it. My only regret is that some of these nostalgic early settlers didn't hail from countries where the birds were a little more colourful. The scarlet or gold of some orioles and tanagers would do a lot to brighten up our dreary winter mornings.

From Kawakawa Bay it is not far to Miranda and here can be seen one of the most impressive assemblages of wading birds in Aotearoa. Godwits, knots, dotterels and plovers all spend at least part of the year here, while a number of very rare visitors to our shores have also turned up at Miranda. There is an excellent educational centre at Miranda and this is of considerable assistance to visitors – even those people who, like me, have difficulty in telling one wader from another. In the hills behind Miranda, at Mangatawhiri, you have a fair chance of seeing galahs.

From Miranda, the return trip to Auckland can be made via the Hunua Ranges and these can be reached by turning inland at Miranda and then continuing on through Mangatangi and Moumoukai. The Hunuas cover more than 25,000 ha and, although not quite as rich in vegetation as the Waitakere Ranges, around 300 species of trees and plants have been found here. It was also until recently the only place near Auckland where the kokako was still found and they were in very small numbers, about four or five birds, when rigorous pest control measures were introduced. At last count there were about 500 pairs, a truly remarkable achievement. Other natives still found in this area include kereru, tui, and the common smaller species; if you are fortunate you might even see kaka or korimako.

Even if only passing through Auckland, you must take time to explore some of the nearby islands of the Hauraki Gulf, many of which are now free of introduced predatory mammals and have translocated populations of rare birds that have largely or completely disappeared from the mainland.

A visit to the island sanctuary of Tiritiri Matangi, located not far off

Auckland's North Shore is a highlight. Tiritiri has an historic lighthouse and was once mostly farmed, but is in the process of being restored to coastal forest. Volunteer groups have planted over 300,000 native trees and eventually much of the island will be forested. To those accustomed to the glorious mix and match of primeval native forest, it is a little unusual to see regimented rows of planted pohutukawa. Still, given time, this hair transplant look will disappear as the tree canopies mature and coalesce.

Translocated native birds include little spotted kiwi (kiwi pukupuku), takahe, brown teal (pateke), red-crowned parakeets (kakariki), rifleman (titipounamu), whiteheads (popokatea), robins (toutouwai), stitchbirds (hihi), kokako and saddlebacks (tieke). Reintroduced reptiles include tuatara and Duvaucel's geckos. Spotless crakes, kereru, tui, bellbirds and the more common smaller bush birds still occurred naturally on Tiritiri when the restoration work began, along with little penguins (korora), grey-faced petrels and diving petrels (kuaka).

This is one of the very few places where you can now conveniently see the tieke in the wild. It moves through the bush with a rapid, almost frenetic motion, seldom pausing in its search for food. Ornithologist Dr Reginald Oliver described the related South Island species as: *...a noisy, active bird progressing by what may be described as long hops or short flights. It appears on the scene to the accompaniment of its shrill notes, moves restlessly about for a few moments and disappears as quickly as it came.*

Anyone watching the tieke for any length of time would probably think it too quick for any predator to catch, but its roosting and nesting habits were its undoing. It spends the night on low perches on or near ground level and nests in holes easily accessible to foraging rats. DoC workers have been trying to condition it to use nestboxes, but maybe it is a little optimistic to try and cram a few million years of evolution into a couple of lifetimes. It will be interesting to see what association the tieke will form with the whitehead now they are both on Tiritiri, as early observers noted that the foraging flocks of whitehead were accompanied by a pair of tieke which acted as guardians of sorts – indeed, they are said to take their name from 'tiaki', the Maori name for guardian.

Another accessible island well worth visiting either by sea or air, is Great Barrier. Called Aotea (the long, white cloud) in Maori, this rugged island was once home to kokako but sadly these are now gone, probably wiped out by high numbers of introduced ship rats. However, the island is free of possums and mustelids and, since it lacks these important predators, has good numbers of banded rails and kaka. The island is also a stronghold for brown teal (pateke), and it holds the larger of just two remaining colonies of the rare black or Parkinson's petrel (takoketai). The extensive wetlands on the eastern side support abundant fernbird populations and a few Australasian bitterns, while the ocean beaches and dunelands have breeding New Zealand dotterels and variable oystercatchers.

The island was once covered in extensive stands of kauri, but only small areas now remain. One of the largest sawmills in the Southern Hemisphere once operated on the Barrier and kauri logs were floated in for milling from the Coromandel and even from the Bay of Islands. Today, the only remnants of the mill's activities are kauri wharf pilings and some old dams, the largest of which was swept away in 2014 in a big storm. Following years of logging and burning, manuka and kanuka forest and scrublands have regenerated over most of the formerly cleared areas. From 1955 the Forest Service carried out trial plantings of kauri with a view to establishing commercial plantations. However, the planting of kauri ceased some years ago. More recently, these plantings and natural stands of kauri have become threatened by kauri dieback disease.

Whaling, too, figured prominently in the island's early and more recent Pakeha history. Because of its position along a humpback migration route, the whales were easily caught by motorised catchers, which operated from Whangaparapara between 1956 and 1962. Being close to major migration routes has also meant that the Barrier has been a significant site for whale strandings. In fact, one of our largest recorded strandings of 450 pilot whales took place at Dawa Bay, on the Barrier, in 1985.

Much closer to Auckland and a short ferry ride from the city is Rangitoto. Formed by a volcanic eruption which started about 600 years ago, Rangitoto is today covered with regenerating pohutukawa forest, together with mapou, mahoe, kanuka, puriri and kohekohe, along with over 40 species of ferns. Also on Rangitoto are quite extensive stands of rata, some of which have hybridised with pohutukawa, much to the fascination of botanists. Possums and wallabies once occurred here and on adjoining Motutapu Island in large numbers, but were exterminated during the 1990s. This was followed by a successful project, completed in 2011, to eradicate the remaining pest mammals. Following removal of mammalian predators the birdlife has bounced back. Pateke, kaka, kakariki and bellbirds have recolonised the islands naturally while brown kiwi, takahe, shore plover (tuturuatu), whiteheads and saddlebacks have been reintroduced. Before pest eradication the birdlife was much like the mainland and dominated by the usual more common native and introduced species. There is a large colony of black-backed gulls on the southern side of Rangitoto, and little penguins, variable oystercatchers and New Zealand dotterels breed along the coasts of both islands.

Nearby Motuihe Island is also in the process of ecological restoration and well worth a visit. All pest mammals have been removed and large areas of coastal forest have been planted. A range of the more common native bush birds are present and these have been supplemented by translocations of little spotted kiwi, red-crowned kakariki, whiteheads, bellbirds and saddlebacks. Tuatara and several lizard species have also been released there.

The jewel of the islands, in conservation terms, is undoubtedly Little Barrier. Known as Hauturu-o-Toi in Maori, it was occupied at the time of Pakeha settlement by a few members of the Ngati Manuhiri people. After the island was gazetted by the government as a sanctuary 'for the preservation of native fauna' in 1895, the few Maori still living on Hauturu were evicted in what can only be described as a very shabby manner. Here alone, however, the stitchbird (hihi) survived, despite strenuous efforts by introduced cats, and bird collectors such as Andreas Reischek to exterminate it. Reischek visited the island five times during the early 1880s and collected some 150 stitchbirds, knowing that they had already disappeared from the mainland. Cook's and black petrels also breed here, but their numbers were depleted by both feral cats and kiore, the only predatory mammals that reached Hauturu. Feral cats were finally exterminated by the Wildlife Service in 1980, and kiore in an aerial poison drop carried out by the Department of Conservation in 2004. This has allowed the birds, including the burrowing petrels, to make a comeback.

The removal of cats has also allowed a number of endangered birds to be released on Hauturu. The first of these was kokako in 1981, which were rescued from native forests being clear-felled at the time on the Volcanic Plateau. Kokako were followed by kakapo in 1982 and saddlebacks in 1984. The kokako and saddlebacks have thrived and their populations on Hauturu now number in the hundreds and thousands respectively. Kakapo did not do so well, and during the late 1990s all known birds were transferred back to Codfish/Whenua Hou and other southern islands, which more closely met their requirements. Several very successful kakapo breeding years followed, which enabled a number of birds to be returned to Hauturu from 2012. Also on Hauturu is the only known breeding colony of the NZ storm petrel (takahikare raro) which was rediscovered in 2003 after being 'lost' for over a century. The breeding site on Hauturu was only discovered after radio-tagged birds caught at sea were tracked back to their nesting burrows. How this tiny storm petrel managed to survive and breed on Hauturu alongside predatory feral cats and kiore is a mystery.

With a regular ferry service from Downtown Auckland, Waiheke Island is the most easily reached of all the Gulf islands and the western end is like a bushy suburb of Auckland. Of all the islands it is probably the least interesting for the naturalist; however, the local community has recently established a restoration project, Te Korowai o Waiheke, which aims to free Waiheke of most predatory mammals. Along with weka, kaka have recently recolonised the island and now breed in several places, including the Forest and Bird Reserve at Onetangi. If you have a few hours to spare, take a walk northwards from the ferry wharf at Matiatia and enjoy spectacular coastal views along Te Ara Hura, the track which encircles much of Waiheke. Little penguins nest in sea caves along the rocky coast, and at one point during summer, there is a bird's eye view over a white-fronted tern colony. From the main centre in Oneroa a short walk down Tui Street takes you to Blackpool Beach, where there is a high tide roost with bar-tailed godwits, both species of oystercatchers and New Zealand dotterels. For longer bush walks, Whakanewha Regional Park at Rocky Bay has a network of tracks through mature and regenerating coastal forest.

Finally, and not to be missed in Auckland, are the flocks of migratory shorebirds which turn up annually near Mangere Bridge. Here in the winter months at high tide, on a drive along Kiwi Esplanade, thousands of South Island pied oystercatchers, or SIPOs to birders, along with a small number of variable oystercatchers, or VOCs, can be seen roosting on the grassy seaside reserve. With their striking black and white plumage, believe me, it's impossible to miss them.

The Manukau Harbour holds New Zealand's greatest numbers of shorebirds and is one of the best places to see the endemic wrybill, a species much coveted by twitchers. Wrybills only number about 5,000 birds in total and about half of the global population winters in the Manukau. One of the best shorebird viewing spots in the Manukau is along the foreshore of Ambury Regional Park, where a viewing hide provides a great vantage point across some nearby man-made shellbank roosts. Huge flocks of shorebirds gather here at high tide. In late summer there are usually several thousand bar-tailed godwits (kuaka) and red knots (huahou), along with thousands of pied oystercatchers and hundreds of wrybills and pied stilts. Other shorebirds include royal spoonbills, white-faced herons, New Zealand dotterels, turnstones, Caspian terns, gulls and some of the rarer Arctic visitors such as whimbrel, eastern curlew and sandpipers. As the tide falls, the wrybills move onto the exposed mud near the roost, where they scythe through the surface ooze with their sideways-twisted bills.

If you are not sure what you are looking at, ask one of the local birders who often visit armed with binoculars and powerful telescopes. The hide is easily reached from the Ambury Regional Park car park by following the road past the park buildings. At the gate turn left along the coastal walkway and follow the signs to the bird hide. If you have a bike you can ride for several kilometres along the coastal walkway to the historic Otuataua Stonefields.

CHAPTER 3

Waikato, Rotorua & Taupo/The Volcanic Plateau

The boundary between Auckland and the Waikato is marked by the Bombay Hills, which lie 45 km south of the city centre. Bombay itself, named after an immigrant ship, is a small farming community in an area dedicated to market gardening. As you drive through this area it is difficult to imagine when looking at the neatly tended fields and rows of vegetables that it is only just over 150 years since widescale settlement began. Then, apart from some fern-covered land cleared by Maori, this entire region was covered by forest, with kauri dominating the higher reaches and kahikatea the lower, more swampy areas. Now it's mostly cabbages, cauliflower and bok choy, though increasingly competing with a desire for new housing developments.

As well as the birds, such as greenfinches, goldfinches, yellowhammers, thrushes and blackbirds, there are also white cockatoos, although not in the numbers in which they occur in the hills to the west around Port Waikato. Another recent arrival to the Bombay Hills is that bane of the Australian wheat farmer, the galah. How these pretty pink and grey parrots got here no one seems to know. They could be wind-blown strays from across the Tasman or perhaps aviary escapees like the rosella.

Continue south and you will reach the Waikato proper. Here, and at the Waikato River itself, is a series of lakes and some of the most important wetlands of the North Island. The Waikato is our longest river at 354 km and was of major importance to Maori as it allowed easy passage by canoe to many parts of the country. Originally the Waikato entered the Pacific Ocean via the Hauraki Gulf but millions of years ago it changed direction – apparently as a result of a volcanic eruption – and began to flow into the Manukau Harbour. Finally it broke through the coastal hills further south and now flows into the Tasman Sea near Port Waikato.

The various eruptions of Taupo to the south dumped massive amounts of pumice into the Waikato River, blocking it and causing it to overflow its banks and change course. From a point at Piarere, between Tirau and Cambridge, the river has sometimes flowed north down the Hinuera Valley past Matamata, and at other times travelled through the Karapiro Gorge and then past Cambridge.

After leaving the Karapiro Gorge the Waikato dumped huge amounts of sediment in a fan across the floor of what is now called the Hamilton Basin. Over time the river has taken different courses across the fan and in its wake it has left sand and gravel levees, or natural stopbanks. These have blocked the drainage of the plains, forming lakes and wetlands.

Chief among these wetlands is the Whangamarino Wetland, now separated from the river itself. Some 7,000 ha in area, it is exceeded in size in the top half of the North Island only by the Kopuatai Peat Dome on the Hauraki Plains. To reach Whangamarino take the turn-off off SH1 to Te Kauwhata. This is clearly signposted about 70 km south of Auckland. At the first hill a good view can be had of Lake Waikare on the right and Whangamarino is straight ahead and off to the left.

Just after passing through Te Kauwhata a no exit road called Swan Road leads off to the left, ending at the Raeo arm of the swamp. This area is popular with North Island fernbirds (koroatito) as well as with bitterns (matuku hurepo) and although the cryptic colouration of these birds makes them hard to spot, their foghorn-like booms can be clearly heard on summer evenings.

Returning from Swan Road take the road to Waerenga which will bring you to the second major southern extension of the swamp. About 4 km on, this road crosses the Lake Waikare Outlet Canal and the second road to the left past this is Falls Road, leading to Island Block and Kopuku. A bridge across the Whangamarino River is 6 km further down this road and the swamp beside the bridge is prime waterfowl/puwaiwai habitat. However, ever increasing numbers of koi carp are now a major pest as they stir up the stream and lake beds and predate native fish and crustacea.

The Whangamarino Wetlands once earned adverse publicity because of large parts being burned off in feuds between marijuana growers. In the fires, large numbers of chicks of rare species such as the bittern perished along with species such as fernbirds which are weak flyers. Survivors were forced to move into parts of the swamp occupied by other birds, so the chances of their survival were poor.

Department of Conservation (DoC) officials estimated that approximately one-third of the 9,000 fernbirds in the swamp died in the fires and although 6,000 birds of one species might seem a healthy remnant, it must be remembered that these birds now survive only in small areas of swamp and are highly vulnerable. Also, even birds such as the spotless and marsh crakes and the banded rails which probably escaped the fires had a greatly reduced habitat.

It was not only birds that suffered. Some of our rarest rushes and ferns grew at Whangamarino and botanists feared that it would take many years for the damaged habitats to fully recover.

However, there are substantial parts of the wetlands that escaped unscathed and these provide shelter and feeding grounds for large flocks of waterbirds. Mallards and grey ducks and their hybrids, are the most common with a population estimated at around 100,000 birds. There are also some 5,000 black swans found here, along with lesser numbers of grey teal, shovelers, black shags and pied stilt.

These birds are also in reasonable numbers in other wetlands, as well as in the lakes along the Waikato River. Not far from the Whangamarino Wetlands are the lakes of Rotokawau, Kopuera, Whangape, Waahi, Ohinewai, Rotongaro and Hakanoa, all fringing the present or former courses of the Waikato, and the combined waterfowl population of this area is probably more than a million birds. These numbers, naturally, fluctuate wildly in the shooting season, when the more prudent waterbirds take their annual vacations at urban lakes and ponds.

The Waikato River itself might seem to be a prime habitat, but introduced alder and three types of willows which have taken over many of the swamps now dominate all the river banks making them unsuitable for the breeding of many species. Shags, however, find the willows ideal for nesting and roosting and there are a number of shaggeries here.

South of the wetlands one finds the farmlands that typify the Waikato. The 'Europeanisation' of the Waikato landscape means that one can drive through much of it without seeing a native bird and very seldom a native tree. However, the introduced trees now growing here are often much larger than the same types in their countries of origin. Avenues of poplars and planes and groves of oaks give parts of the Waikato a park-like appearance.

Just over 50 km past the Te Kauwhata turn-off on SH1 is Hamilton, administrative and commercial centre of the Waikato. Hamilton has its fair share of colourful trees, including a flowering gum in Princes Street and some particularly fine trees line the beautiful riverside paths. A trip on the river on a tourist boat will help visitors appreciate their beauty.

Moving south of Hamilton along SH1 and through some of our most fertile farmlands brings you to Cambridge. This area was once mostly covered in forest but after the land was confiscated from Maori during the New Zealand Wars widescale clearance began and today only small pockets of forest remain around Mount Pirongia and Maungatautari Mountain or the remoter areas south of Port Waikato.

One of the major conservation successes in Aotearoa in recent years has been the creation of Sanctuary Mountain Maungatautari. This is a fenced predator-proof enclosure which has been constructed around the upper section of Mt Maungatautari. It is situated at 99 Tari Rd, Pukeatua about 30 minutes drive from Cambridge. The fence, which at 47 km is one of the world's longest, encloses 3,400 ha of conifer/broadleaf/podocarp forest which has been cleared of predators and herbivores. This has resulted in a steadily increasing community of birds many of which have gone from forests elsewhere including kokako, tieke, North Island robins (toutouwai), whitehead (popokatea) as well as the Western race of the North Island brown kiwi. There are also giant weta, tuatara and various lizards.

One of the most interesting successes is that the understorey and the sub-canopy of the forest recovered remarkably quickly after herbivores, particularly deer, goats and possums were removed and a lot of plants, now mostly gone from other North Island forests are now flourishing.

The road from Cambridge to Rotorua is an easy drive through interesting country. Karapiro, about 8 km south of Cambridge, is a good spot for watching waterbirds. If you haven't seen the little diving duck, the black teal or scaup, so far in your travels, you might well see it here. It is essentially a lake and pond dweller and rapidly colonised the lakes created by the hydro-electric dams within months of their being filled.

Travelling towards Rotorua one leaves the farmlands of the Waikato and moves into the Mamaku Ranges. Farming in this area started late because of a wasting disease affecting all livestock. This was eventually found to be caused by cobalt and selenium deficiencies in the soil. Once this was corrected by topdressing, settlement by Pakeha was rapid, and large areas, particularly to the south, are now in dry stock or dairying.

The Mamaku Plateau was built up by a series of volcanic eruptions which threw up tremendous quantities of fragmental rhyolitic debris that coalesced on landing into a coherent, massive rock called ignimbrite. Ignimbrite landscapes are very distinctive and the Mamaku plateau is one of the most outstanding of these. Geological opinion is divided as to whether the Plateau is made up of separate types of ignimbrite, or one type divided into sections.

Extensive forests remain in the north of the Mamakus but this has probably more to do with the difficulty of turning it into pasture than any deliberate conservation policy. Nevertheless, in the remoter areas there still exist good stands of rimu, miro, tawa, hinau, rewarewa, mangeao, totara and kahikatea together with various types of beech.

To see most of this forest requires forays on foot but for those who are either in a hurry, or not energetic, there is a particularly fine patch of bush astride SH5, the main road from Hamilton to Rotorua, at Fitzgerald Glade. You could not ask for a better example of the riotous proliferation of undergrowth where browsing animals are excluded.

Together with the forested ranges to the east this area is known collectively as the Kaimai-Mamakus. This bush has quite a variety of native birds: kaka, robins, tits, tui and korimako are sometimes found here, along with the occasional whitehead and rifleman. Most notably, the area boasts one of the country's largest populations of kokako.

The kokako was one of New Zealand's most endangered birds. In fact, with the possible exception of the kakapo, it is difficult to think of a bird more afflicted with evolutionary limitations. It is an indifferent flyer so cannot move from forest that is being logged; it needs an extensive area of bush to maintain a viable population; it feeds on the ground so is vulnerable to attack from stoats, ferrets and feral cats; possum and deer both compete with it for food; and when it attempts its dawn chorus where the bush is close to open country, such as the Rangitoto Range, it is mobbed by magpies.

Even today the kokako's habitat is under threat. A number of years ago, the corridor linking the population of about 100 birds in the East Mamakus with the 200 in the West Mamakus, probably then the country's largest remaining viable population, was strip-felled of trees for paper pulp. Moves are underway to get this corridor replanted, but regeneration of trees takes years and time is one thing the kokako doesn't have.

After leaving the Kaimai-Mamakus one passes through the farmlands around Ngongotaha before reaching Rotorua. About 5 km from Rotorua on SH5 is the National Kiwi Hatchery Aotearoa. It runs regular tours and if you are interested in the sterling work being carried out to assist in the survival of our national icon it's well worth a visit.

Rotorua, famous for its thermal wonders and scenic lakes, is the North Island's premier tourist attraction. The city of Rotorua is situated on the southern shores of Lake Rotorua, on comparatively flat land with hills rising off to the south and west. The lake, some 10 km in diameter, was at one time considerably larger with a level 100 m above its present one. But wander only a short distance from the typical tourist habitat and there is plenty to see and do. A stone's throw from downtown Rotorua, on a steaming silica spit in Sulphur Bay, is the largest colony of black-billed gulls in the North Island, far from their usual nesting areas in Canterbury's braided riverbeds. The warm, murky, sulphurous water is so acidic that long-term residents often have the webs of their feet missing, dissolved by constant immersion in the water. Also nesting there are red-billed gulls and little black shags.

Although both red-billed and black-billed gulls nest in the same area, their habits differ considerably. Red-billed gulls are unabashed scroungers who frequent the Rotorua rubbish tip and 'work' the tourists along the nearby lakefront. Black-bills, with southern decorum, eschew such common behaviour, 'follow the plow' and forage in pastures in surrounding farmlands.

These gulls also feature in the history of the local Arawa people. In 1823 during an attack by the Ngapuhi from north of Auckland, the Arawa, who were ensconced on Mokoia Island, were alerted by the calls of the gulls. The belief arose that the souls of the Arawa killed in the ensuing battle entered the gulls and they were thereafter protected by a tapu.

Here, as in the Waikato, exotic trees flourish, and the stand of redwoods at Whakarewarewa is considered to be the finest outside their native California. This stand was the most successful of a number of experimental plots planted in 1901 in various parts of the country. Other fine examples are to be found at Hamurana Springs on the northern shore of the lake.

The cold springs of Hamurana, Rainbow and Fairy Springs and the hot springs of Whakarewarewa, Kuirau and Ohinemutu all feed into Lake Rotorua and these have been developed into popular tourist facilities.

There are some 20 lakes within 30 km of the town, all of volcanic origin and filling craters, calderas and valleys blocked off by lava flows. Although some of these are small and relatively inaccessible, there are a number of particularly beautiful lakes within easy reach of the city.

To the east of Rotorua are Rotoiti, Rotoehu and Rotoma. These are popular with anglers for their rainbow trout but they are also fringed with forest which supports good numbers of birds. All are easily reached from SH30, although this road winds quite a bit, particularly near Lake Rotoiti, so should be treated with respect.

The road to Lake Okataina leaves SH30 at Ruato, 22 km east of Rotorua. This is probably the most beautiful of all Rotorua's lakes, a gem in a sylvan setting.

I will always remember as a child being shown the lair of a feral cat near Lake Okataina. Besides the sad remains of a range of exotic birds we also found those of fantails, pied tits, warblers and robins. At least 50 birds had been killed by this cat to feed her kittens and although this particular brood was disposed of, there are many more thousands throughout the country and the damage they do is tremendous. The feral cat (tori) is a bigger and more rangy animal than its domestic antecedents and although usually a tabby it sometimes has traces of other forebears as well.

Despite the ravages of these predators, native birds manage to survive in the Rotorua area. The bellbird is doing well even though it has disappeared from many other areas, possibly because of a disease introduced by exotic birds. Bellbirds (korimako) from Rotorua have been used to restock other areas, including Waiheke Island off Auckland. They are particularly partial to the native fuchsia (kotukutuku) so look for them where these are flowering.

Not surprisingly, with the numbers of lakes and swamps in this area waterfowl are plentiful. Scaup (papango) occur in scattered groups along the margins of most lakes as do black swans, mallards and grey duck and recently, a small group of chestnut-breasted shelducks were seen on Lake Rotorua. Although similar to our paradise shelduck, they can be distinguished by the black heads of both sexes. One of the main populations of the rare NZ dabchick (weweia) is to be found here and they can often be seen around Mokoia Island, on Lake Rotorua, and on Lake Rotoiti. NZ scaup nested in many of the burial caves of this island, which offered particularly effective protection for them, given the respect in which Maori have always held for the dead. The white-eyed duck (karakahia) was once common on Lake Rotomahana but was apparently wiped out in the volcanic eruption of Mt Tarawera in 1886.

Travel south or west of Rotorua and it is difficult to see anything but exotic trees. In the last 80 or so years vast areas have been planted in exotics and more than 50,000 ha of this is in radiata pine with smaller plantings of Corsican pine, Ponderosa pine, Douglas fir and other species such as eucalypts. The Kaingaroa Forest, to the south-east, covering some 138,000 ha, was once the

largest planted forest on Earth with kilometre after kilometre of road lined with similar-sized trees. It is hard to imagine anything more different from the coniferous forests in places like Scandinavia where the trees grow in a beautiful variety of species and sizes.

About 20 km south of Rotorua on SH5 is a junction with a loop road going to the Waimangu Valley, and a track leading on to Lake Rotomahana. This whole area was devastated by the Tarawera eruption and the later explosion of the Waimangu Geyser and now boasts the largest boiling lake in the world with a fauna adapted to the extreme conditions.

From Waimangu continuing down the loop road will bring you out on to SH38 to Kaingaroa. Three kilometres down this route the road leading off to the left will take you around the north of Lake Rerewhakaaitu and along the access road to the approaches to Mt Tarawera, the scene of the most devastating volcanic eruption in the last two hundred years.

On 10 June 1886, with virtually no warning, Tarawera erupted, killing 153 people, devastating a huge area of the central North Island and destroying the settlements of Te Ariki and Te Wairoa. The famed Pink and White Terraces, the 'marvels of natural architecture', made up of shining silica, were completely destroyed and Lake Rotomahana itself was formed in the eruption.

Most of the Rotorua-Tarawera district was covered in scrub and fern before the eruption, with tall forest covering the lower flanks of Rainbow Mountain, and much of this, particularly near the centre of the blast, was destroyed. Today, the vegetation on the lower slopes is regenerating, but a series of nine gigantic craters are as raw and stark as the day they were formed and all around them the land is bare.

Back on SH5, Waiotapu provides an easily accessible thermal area. The inhabitants of the streams there do not always avoid hot water and red freshwater crayfish are a common sight. Mosses and lichens grow in sharply defined areas, each adapting to the great variations in heat, acidity and soil type.

After passing through the pine forests one again reaches farming country and then, a few kilometres north of Lake Taupo, the geothermal field at

Wairakei. Besides thermal activity, Wairakei is of interest for the unusual life it supports. Swallows drift through the steam and several endemic plants grow here that are not found elsewhere. Among these is a rare thermophile ladder fern, *Nephrolepis flexuosa,* a large colony of which was destroyed by nearby tourist development. Yet another fern, *Christella dentata* was lost after the water level dropped when steam was extracted for the geothermal field. It has, however, established new colonies where bores have been sunk to maintain water temperatures.

Almost opposite Wairakei are the Huka Falls, the most spectacular falls in the country. Acting as a natural barrier, they prevented eels and other fish species from reaching Lake Taupo so that when Pakeha arrived the lake was virtually empty of fish. It certainly didn't remain so for long. By 1885 the Auckland Acclimatisation Society had released trout in the lake with phenomenal success, reaching a thousand tonnes a year. At one time trout were so plentiful they were given to farmers for use as pig food. Of interest too, are the colonies of exotic aquarium fish such as guppies, swordtails and mollies, which are now living in thermal areas.

The lake itself gained its present form in an eruption around the year AD 186. This explosion was so great that its atmospheric after-effects were mentioned in both Chinese and Roman chronicles of the time. It also destroyed much of the original dense forest that stretched over the central North Island.

The land around the lake was covered in layers of pumice thrown out by the eruptions and most of this today supports only scrub. When the Pakeha arrived the land to the north of Lake Taupo was mostly clear of larger vegetation and the Waikato missionary, the Rev. Benjamin Y. Ashwell, one of the first Pakeha to travel through this area, has left a vivid description of what he saw:

> *The country was desolate beyond description. Thousands of thousands of acres of miserable land without Tree or Shrub. Water also was scarce. This plain extends to Taupo, Rotorua and almost to Ahuriri. I was forcibly reminded of the great and terrible wilderness spoken of in Scripture.*

One of the more surprising features that the Pakeha explorers noted was the presence of pohutukawa here. Although this tree is usually coastal, it is thought that saplings were brought from the coast. These ancient trees still grow on Motutaiko Island in Lake Taupo and the name Motutaiko is also of interest to the travelling naturalist as it means 'island of the petrel'. This means that nesting petrels would have commuted to the sea nightly in order to feed their chicks, a round trip of quite a few hundred kilometres. If there is a contender for the hardest working seabird parents I would plump for these taiko.

Except for an area where the Tongariro and Tokaanu rivers meet near Turangi, the lake is too deep to support many birds as they are unable to reach the bottom to feed. At Taupo, a few mallards and swans loiter about waiting for handouts, and there are shags like the little shag which fish for a living. The white-faced heron and rare reef heron turn up fairly regularly, the latter being particularly fascinating to watch as it fishes. While waiting for a fish to come within range, it holds its wings up and forward, forming a parasol, shading the water so that it can see more clearly. Then suddenly its head shoots forward to catch an unlucky fish.

One of our rarer waterbirds, the NZ dabchick, is still found in reasonable numbers to the south of Lake Taupo and the recent immigrant, the Australian coot, has started breeding on the lake. Taupo also boasts some unusual bird records, including an amokura, a red-tailed tropical bird, which was taken alive here in 1936.

In those areas around Taupo that escaped the devastation of the eruption around AD186, trees have flourished. A giant totara found by a deerstalker in April 1978 in the Hauhungaroa Range west of Lake Taupo is one of the country's finest and about 2,000 years old. Also one of the largest rimu in New Zealand is to be found several hundred metres from the north-eastern boundary of the Pikiariki Ecological Area in the Pureora Forest Park. Ironically, it was spared from being logged because it was too big for the local mill to handle. At Turangi it is possible to book raft trips on the Tongariro River where you have a good chance of seeing the beautiful blue duck or whio.

Above the treeline higher areas not under tussock are covered with tutu,

Raoulia and Danthonia. The tree tutu, *Coriaria arborea*, contains a toxin called tutin, responsible over the years for the deaths of many sheep and cattle. Horses seem to have sense enough not to eat it and goats can get away with eating just about anything, but some early settlers claimed to have lost up to a quarter of their livestock from 'toot' poisoning.

Humans have also fallen foul of tutu: an outbreak of honey poisoning in the 1940s was traced to honeydew from this plant and since then the making of honey in certain areas where tutu is prevalent is illegal. The tutu poison tutin is suprisingly lethal and has even killed elephants. One of these fatalities occurred in this area in 1956 when a circus elephant ate tutu while being watered in the Mangawhero River. It is buried at Ohakune Junction.

On clear days, particularly in winter, beautiful Mt Tongariro is clearly visible from most parts of the lake. Tongariro is the site of New Zealand's first national park, created from 2,600 ha of land gifted to the nation in 1887 by the Tuwharetoa chief Te Heuheu Tukino. It is centred around three often-active volcanoes, Tongariro, Ngauruhoe and Ruapehu, and one of the most popular of our parks with over one milliom visitors recorded in a year. Many visitors come to ski the North Island's most popular ski fields – Turoa and Whakapapa on Mt Ruapehu.

Adjacent to the Tongariro National Park is the Tongariro State Forest which is regenerating after being heavily logged of rimu, matai, totara and kahikatea in the years up to 1977. The once-splendid stands of totara were badly affected, although other species such as kaikawaka and matai can still be found in good numbers. Blue duck or whio are found in the higher reaches of the Whanganui, the Manganuiateao and the Whakapapa rivers which drain the forest. Kiwi and morepork (ruru) are both heard at night and the noisy calls of the kaka are often the first sound heard on waking – if one gets to sleep at all.

The Kaimanawa Forest Park, covering almost 75,000 ha of the Kaimanawa Ranges, lies to the south-east of Lake Taupo. Covered by snow in winter, the park consists of a variety of terrain including forested river valleys, extensive scrubland and upland tussock. Beech forest covers much of the park but this gives way to podocarp forest in the north-west. Fires in the south during both Maori and early Pakeha periods destroyed some of the forest which has now been replaced by tussock, scrub and in some areas herbfields.

In the forested areas of the Kaimanawas most of the more common bush birds occur along with riflemen, whiteheads and long-tailed cuckoos. The whitehead and the brown creeper are favourite hosts for the eggs of the cuckoo and their disappearance from many areas has probably caused it to seek out other birds. Tui and bellbirds react strongly to the presence of this bird and vigorously mob it.

Wild pigs, red deer and the only wild herd of sika deer in the Southern Hemisphere occur here and in the neighbouring Kaweka Forest Park, but what distinguishes the Kaimanawas is the presence of approximately several hundred wild horses along the Moawhango River. The horses have been here for more than a century and have developed characteristics similar to those of wild horses of Britain and Europe. Their adaptations to their environment are of scientific interest and the horses are strictly protected.

The Moawhango Ecological District itself is situated in an area bounded by the Tongariro volcanoes and the Kaimanawa and Kaweka Ranges to the north and the Ruahine Ranges to the east. It is of special interest to botanists because around 150 plants, otherwise restricted to the South Island high country, are found here. There are also striking scenic similarities to parts of the South Island, such as the Matiri Plateau in north-west Nelson and parts of Central Otago. Much of the original forest which covered an area from Waiouru to the Ruahines was destroyed by fire some 600 years ago. As a result most of this land was in mixed scrub and tussock until converted to clover and rye grass by settlers.

The name Moawhango can be translated variously as 'the hoarse call of the moa' or as 'many moa', and is one of the few places where this bird's name has been preserved.

Oral tradition lasts only a few generations and in consequence once birds disappear their names often follow them into oblivion. One of the lesser sorrows of the extinction of so many species, but a sorrow nevertheless, is the disappearance of the charming Maori names, as scientific names often sound unwieldy at best, or pretentious at worst. Of the 'kararehe whenua', the original fauna, the names (and some bones) are all that remain of the moa, hokioi (eagle), tarepo (goose) and kawekaweau (giant skink).

CHAPTER 4

King Country/Te Rohe Potae and Taranaki

The King Country is named after the movement King Tawhiao led last century to resist alienation of Maori land. After the movement's failure, he and his followers sought refuge in the remoter parts of this region and for a time thereafter Pakeha ventured into the King Country at their peril. Although the King Country now has several substantial towns, beyond them a sense of isolation persists in what is some of the North Island's wildest terrain.

Because of suspicion of Pakeha intentions it was not until the turn of this century that Pakeha settlement and farming of the King Country really began and it was the completion of the North Island main trunk line in 1908 that accelerated this development.

After the First World War, thousands of servicemen came home looking for land, but only rugged forested areas such as the King Country were available. They were entitled to an advance of £5,000 to buy land and a further £1,000-£2,000 to develop it, but this proved inadequate for many attempting to settle in the King Country. Kenneth Cumberland, the noted geographer, best summed up their plight when he wrote:

> *Many of the buyers and lessees in this frantic rush for land found themselves on rough hill country, in virgin bush, remote, isolated and without roads. Many of the soldier-settlers were underequipped, undercapitalised and lacking in experience, on land overvalued and heavily mortgaged. And all were relying, without question, on a continuation of boom prices for what they hoped to be able to produce.*

The collapse of prices for primary produce in 1921, combined with the high cost of loan repayments, and the effort required in keeping the cleared land free of regenerating bush and fertilised, were in the end the downfall of many would-be farmers. Large areas of land were abandoned and although there was a resurgence of interest after the Second World War, when the advent of aerial topdressing greatly reduced development costs, farming in much of the King Country has never been economically viable.

Driving south on SH3, Otorohanga is the first main town you will see, 29 km from Te Awamutu. It boasts the Kiwi House and Native Bird Park on Alex Telfer Drive, where you can be sure of seeing kiwi in the excellent nocturnal house. This centre made a name for itself by one of the first places to successfully breed kiwi and it has exported these to several countries.

The park also has one of the best collections of native avifauna in the country. Besides the nocturnal house there is a large walk-through aviary where tui, kereru and other birds can be seen flying around. There is also a good collection of native reptiles, and it has a breeding complex for blue duck (whio). Also being developed is a facility for breeding the Mahoenui giant weta (wetapunga). This is also the only place in Aotearoa where the New Zealand falcon (karearea) has been bred.

Dominating the north of the King Country is Mt Pirongia and this is worth exploring. From Otorohanga take SH31 towards Kawhia and the turn-off left to Pirongia is about 15 km further on. At the Heritage and Information Centre in Pirongia information on the park can be obtained.

Pirongia Forest Park is centred around the mountain of the same name, an abbreviation of Pirongia-te-Aroaro o Kahu (the fragrant presence of Kahu), not kahu the hawk, but Kahupeka the wife of Ue, a tohunga of the Tainui. Superb views can be had from the crest of the mountain on clear days.

The park covers approximately 17,000 ha and most of the forest is in prime condition, albeit a little chewed up by deer and possums. A kahikatea, the largest recorded native tree in the country, grows on the bank of the Kaniwhaniwha Stream which flows through the park. It is 66.5 m tall and it is a 12 km round trip to walk there. I visited it about 10 years ago when there was no easy access and still remember it well.

The park also supports a good selection of native birds among which you might, if lucky, see the kokako and falcon. Tits and robins are also found here but are fairly localised in their distribution. To find out what smaller native birds are present in areas of bush such as this, keep a watch out and listen for calls. There has been a lot of very effective predator control at Pirongia carried out by enthusiastic locals and the kokako and robins which were reintroduced from elsewhere have benefited greatly from this. One female kokako this season had three clutches which may well be a record.

Superb views can be obtained from the crest of the mountain on clear days and one of the best descriptions of this was given by J. Kerry-Nicholls who wrote in his book The King Country published in 1884:

> *When we reached the summit of the mountain, we emerged from the thick forest on to an open spot which commanded a delightful prospect. Turning towards the west, we stood on the brink of a precipice which fell in a clear descent of 1000 feet into the ravine below; here and there a jutting mass of rock stood out in rugged grandeur from the adamantine wall of stone, but otherwise a thick growth of matted scrub covered the sides and bottom of this enormous fissure, and so dense and entangled was the vegetation as we looked down upon it, that it appeared quite possible to walk upon the tops of the trees without falling to the ground. ... . Here and there upon the cultivated flats the white houses of the settlers, embowered who amidst the orchards and gardens, dotted the landscape, while Alexandra, Kihikihi, Hamilton, and Cambridge, and numerous other settlements, served to mark the spots where future cities may ere long grow into existence; and add wealth and prosperity to this fertile land.*

A further 23 km along SH31 from the Pirongia turn-off brings you to Kawhia Harbour. This harbour is one of the country's most important feeding and roosting grounds for wading birds, and here on the sand island in the middle of the lower part of the harbour is a popular roosting area for godwits. It is also the southernmost point on the west coast of New Zealand where pohutukawa first naturally occurred. Black stilt are regularly seen here in winter.

Kawhia Harbour is well known among palaeontologists for its large number of fossils, first found in this area by the German geologist-explorer Dr Ernst

Dieffenbach in 1842. Ammonites and belemnites are particularly plentiful here and the largest ammonite found in New Zealand, a 1.52 m specimen from late Jurassic rocks, was recovered south of the harbour. Although not the largest known, this specimen is still a very respectable size. The belemnites were so common here that Maori children used them as toys believing they were roke kanae, or the excrement of mullet which the fish had left behind on the shore after leaping out of the water.

Back on SH3 one travels 16 km south-west of Otorohanga – 8 km south on SH3, then 8 km off to the right on a well signposted road – to reach the Waitomo Caves. These justly famous caves were formed by underground streams that dissolved passages through the limestone over vast periods. Water percolating through the limestone became charged with lime in solution and, dripping down from the cave roof, left behind deposits which eventually developed into spectacular stalactites and stalagmites. In addition, glow-worms (titiwai) have colonised a number of areas and the boat journey along the underground river through the Glow-worm Grotto is unforgettable.

The best times to visit are early in the morning, soon after opening, and late in the afternoon, when there are fewer tourists. Flooding can cause the glow-worm caves to be closed so, if the weather has been bad, check before going.

Also here is the Waitomo Caves Museum, one of the best small museums in the country. It has an impressive collection of fossils found in the King Country and its dioramas are excellent.

More than 160 King Country caves have provided the fossil remains of 53 land and 2 marine species of birds, many now extinct. From the predominance of forest dwellers among these birds, together with the presence of creatures such as land snails, scientists conclude that from at least 25,000 years ago this area was covered in mixed podocarp-broadleaf forest. The bones of marine birds such as petrels provide evidence that before humans arrived with their mammalian predators these Procellariids bred in the inland forested ranges.

Archaeological evidence also suggests that this is one of the last areas in the North Island where moa survived. They vanished first from the north and then progressively became extinct southwards, and simultaneously from the coast towards the interior.

Research was undertaken in the late 1980s and a sobering list of extinct animals from the area was compiled: 11 moa species, a pelican, a swan, 2 species of geese, 4 duck species, 2 eagle species, a hawk, 5 species of rail, an Aptornis (adzebill), a snipe, an owlet-nightjar, a crow and 3 species of wren – and these are only birds. Indications are that frogs and a lizard might have disappeared too.

Back on SH3, and 12 km south of the Waitomo Caves turn-off, one reaches Te Kuiti and, although most of the birds here are common species, the town does hold one of the country's stranger bird records – a lesser frigatebird which was recovered nearby, a wind-blown tropical stray far from its home range in the central Pacific.

To the south of Te Kuiti's commercial area the road forks and SH30 heads south-east towards Mangakino. Along this road you first pass through farming country, much of which is degenerating into scrub. Paradise shelducks, pied stilts and white-faced herons are all fairly numerous in the damper areas.

A good place to stop is at the Mangaokewa Scenic Reserve which, although a little rugged, supports a number of birds, both native and exotic. Continuing towards Mangakino brings you to Kopaki, named for another of our lost birds, the laughing owl – although the name should more properly be spelt kopake. Also sometimes called whekau in Maori, this bird had developed long, sturdy legs for chasing its prey on foot – most unowl-like behaviour. It ate earthworms, insects, lizards and small birds and is best remembered for its 'doleful shrieks' which were heard incessantly on rainy nights and which were apparently not even remotely like a laugh.

The range of hills known as the Raepahu Range stretching north-east from Kopaki towards the Pureora Forest Park has a good population of birds, including species that are rarities elsewhere like the kakariki and the kaka. The kokako and the falcon (karearea) are also found here and the kokako numbers have seen a massive increase in recent years, due to dedicated predator control measures. At last count there were around 500 birds.

After driving 11 km south of Te Kuiti on SH3 and then taking the SH4 fork, you will come to the next sizeable town of Taumarunui which was once the terminus for launch services up the Wanganui River, but these have been replaced by jet boats. They provide good opportunities to see the birdlife along the river, at their stopping points, although predators have decimated the bird population since the 1920s and 1930s when the launch trips were most popular.

South of Taumarunui the farmland gives way to scrub and bush and then to the tussockland around Waiouru. From here good views can be had of the mountains of Tongariro, Ngauruhoe and Ruapehu across the Rangipo Desert. This countryside supports mostly open country birds such as harriers but black-backed gulls are also seen here sometimes nesting far from the sea, and even NZ dotterels (tuturiwhatu) have been recorded nesting among these bleak surrounds.

To reach New Plymouth from the King Country the usual route is SH3 from Te Kuiti to Piopio and then Awakino. The road passes bush-rimmed gorges, limestone cliffs and several small swamps offering the interested observer a variety of flora and fauna, but nothing particularly rare.

Piopio, like Huia and Moawhanga, is named for a bird now extinct. Some historians say that the name was given to the area by Pakeha settlers, but whatever its origins it sadly commemorates one of our most engaging birds that only relatively recently disappeared.

About 25 km from Piopio, on SH3, is Mahoenui, home of the giant weta or wetapunga *Deinacrida mahoenui*. Wetapunga were once found throughout the mainland but disappeared from most of the country after Pakeha settlement because of the loss of their habitat and also because of predation by rats, stoats, weasels and ferrets. In 1962 a population of the very rare local species of wetapunga was found living in a four hectare patch of gorse at Mahoenui. Although this particular gorse patch was destroyed by fire in 1982, shortly afterwards another colony was found living in a 250 ha patch nearby. Steps have been taken to protect it and the Kiwi House at Otorohanga is setting up a breeding colony.

If you have the time, the route to New Plymouth through Ohura on SH40 is prettier and not as well travelled. Farming in this area is no longer economic and so today Ohura is virtually a ghost town.

This road takes you through the forested ranges of the Waitaanga where all the usual bush birds are found. Kokako were here once but sightings of them have not been recorded in recent years. There are old records of both laughing owls and huia having been seen in the area.

Another route to New Plymouth is from Taumarunui to Whangamomona and then on to Stratford along SH43 and via the beautiful Tangarakau Gorge. Known as the Forgotten World Highway, this route is unusual in that it was once one of the few places where it was possible to hear kokako without leaving the road, but you needed to be a fairly early bird yourself. They have now disappeared. However, robins, tits, fantail and whiteheads are all here in good numbers and it is worthwhile trying to entice them into view.

In New Plymouth itself many of the natural highlights of the city can be conveniently viewed by taking the Te Henui Walkway, which runs along the stream of the same name, not far from the city centre. From this path can be seen some of the fine exotic trees and gardens that grace the city.

Because New Plymouth was one of the first Pakeha settlements in New Zealand, exotic trees are well established. Yet not all of these were planted by the European settlers. The first fruit trees here grew from stones a Maori sailor brought back from Sydney in 1829. By 1841 these were large trees and prolific bearers. At one time exotic tree saplings were grown in Taranaki for export to Australia.

Good stands of native bush – dominated by karaka, kohekohe, tawa and titoki – also grow at several points along the river bank and at certain times of the year these trees are popular with birds, particularly fantails, silvereyes, tui and kereru. The walkway also takes you through several quite extensive patches of open land with livestock and in spring the lambs make these areas look decidedly rustic. Outside the shooting season there are usually paradise shelducks to be seen.

Two reserves in New Plymouth with good collections of exotic trees are the beachside East End Reserve, which is just off SH3 at the mouth of the Te Henui, and the adjoining Brooklands and Pukekura forests on the outskirts of the city.

The two botanical highlights of the East End Reserve are a large Queensland kauri, one of the best examples of this rare tree in New Zealand, and a spectacular bird of paradise plant, with its pale blue flowers offering a pleasing contrast to its banana palm-like foliage.

Besides these, New Plymouth has a number of other parks with good tree collections, both exotic and native. In the adjoining Brooklands and Pukekura Parks on the outskirts of the city are some fine kohekohe, puriri and pukatea and among the exotics are a particularly good gingko tree, a hickory and several excellent pines.

The writer Sir H. Rider Haggard, who was also a connoisseur of trees, estimated one of the Brooklands puriri to be 2,000 years old and one of the world's largest Monterey Pines is growing here.

When the first settlers arrived in Taranaki they found land covered in forest – rimu, miro, totara, kahikatea, pahautea, kamahi, rata, hinau and maire, giving way to beech on the slopes of Mt Taranaki and other higher areas. This was also the southern limit of puriri on the west coast. Now this forest has given way to farmland in the inevitable forest to Friesian cycle.

Inland, the higher reaches are often still well forested and remnant populations of the many seabirds that once bred in the inland ranges still nest here. A colony of grey-faced petrels (oi) can be found near Waireka and a black petrel (taiko) has also been found in Taranaki in recent years.

Immediately offshore from New Plymouth is the Sugar Loaf/Nga Manu Islands Marine Park. Numerous fish are found here together with fur seals which come ashore in the non-breeding season. As the islands are free of rats they are a haven for birds, with around 10,000 seabirds of 9 species nesting here, including black-backed and red-billed gulls, white-fronted terns and at least three types of petrel. The Sugar Loaves themselves are the eroded stumps of what is probably Taranaki's oldest volcano, which was active about one million years ago. Incidentally the 'sugar' is bird poop.

Being one of the westernmost points of the mainland and thus the closest to Australia, Taranaki is often the landing point for wind-blown strays from across the Tasman. The first recorded sightings for spine-tailed swifts were from Taranaki – first at Manaia in 1888 and then at New Plymouth in 1915. They and the related fork-tailed swift still turn up very occasionally in winter.

From everywhere in Taranaki the majestic cone of Mt Taranaki dominates the landscape. Although there is little sign of volcanic activity today, Mt Taranaki should be regarded as dormant rather than extinct. It has been the site of much volcanic activity, the most recent eruption taking place around AD 1775. By volcanic standards this seems to have been fairly mild, but the eruptions that took place around AD 1500 and 1665 were much more violent and most of the vegetation that now clothes the upper areas of the mountain has grown since.

The otherwise perfect symmetry of this mountain is somewhat marred by a ridge on its south-western slopes. This is Fanthams Peak, named for Fanny Fantham who in March 1889, aged 19, became the first woman to climb it.

At various altitudes on Mt Taranaki, differing types of vegetation can be found. The lower slopes have typical broadleaf-podocarp forest and although this appears to be dominated by rata and rimu there are kamahi, mahoe and tree fuchsia as well.

Further up the mountain these trees gradually give way to totara and kaikawaka, the bush in turn giving way to scrub such as leatherwood. Higher up the scrub is replaced by small herbaceous mountain plants. These include some endemic mountain daisies and a rare fern, *Polystichum cystostegia*, which flourishes in rock strewn gullies. A number of roads provide access to the mountain, with walking tracks leading from them. Also on the slopes of the mountain is the Pukeiti Rhododendron Trust, started by Douglas Cook of Eastwoodhill fame, which boasts a fine collection of introduced trees and shrubs.

Yet it was fossils of moa and other birds that attracted a number of early naturalists to the area. In January 1847 Walter Mantell, while searching for moa bones, made a large find of fossils on the southern side of Mt Taranaki.

Among the many moa remains were the bones of a bird at that stage unknown to Europeans, the North Island takahe. Less than a year later this bird was officially described by Dr Richard Owen in London and named after Mantell.

According to Maori tradition, a moa lived on the heights of Mt Taranaki with two giant lizards. In 1839 the German geologist Dr Ernst Dieffenbach, accompanied by two Maori guides, attempted to climb Taranaki. On reaching the snow line, the guides refused to continue. Dieffenbach wrote:

> *The mountains are peopled with mysterious and misshapen animals; the black points, which [the Maori] sees from afar in the dazzling snow are fierce and monstrous birds; a supernatural spirit breathes on him in the evening breeze, or is heard in the rolling of a loose stone.*

Even in recent years there have been reports of birds thought to have been extinct being found alive in the remoter areas of Taranaki. Moa, whekau, piopio, huia and tieke have all been reported, and some of these reports have appeared authentic enough for the authorities to have checked them. In fact, Taranaki was outside the known historical range of the huia, even though there are two place names incorporating 'huia' in the area – Wharehuia (the house of the huia) near Stratford, and Huiakama (nimble huia) on the Whangamomona road, which would seem to indicate they were once found there.

Not to be missed for any interested visitor to Taranaki is the Lake Rotokare Scenic Reserve, 12 km east of the town of Eltham. This is another highly regarded sanctuary which covers 230 ha including the eponymous lake. It is surrounded by an 8.2 km predator-proof fence and 12 pest species have been eradicated. The main trees are tawa, rewarewa and mahoe and there are some fine specimens of kahikatea and pukatea near the lake. Bush birds have thrived since the pest eradiction and tieke and hihi have been reintroduced.

The tieke in particular have flourished with numbers more than quadrupling since they arrived back. Lake Rotokare is another important kiwi creche and has reared good numbers of the western race of the North Island brown kiwi, and kiwi from here have recently been released in the

Kaitaki Range on Mt Taranaki and hopefully they will re-establish. There are good pathways and the lake is worth visiting and you should be able to see some of our native galaxiid fish there. Around the lake there are spotless crake (puweto) and North Island fernbird (koroatito).

Blue duck (whio) have also been reintroduced to Mt Taranaki in recent years and seem to be doing well. They are descendants of captive ducks held and bred mostly in Christchurch.

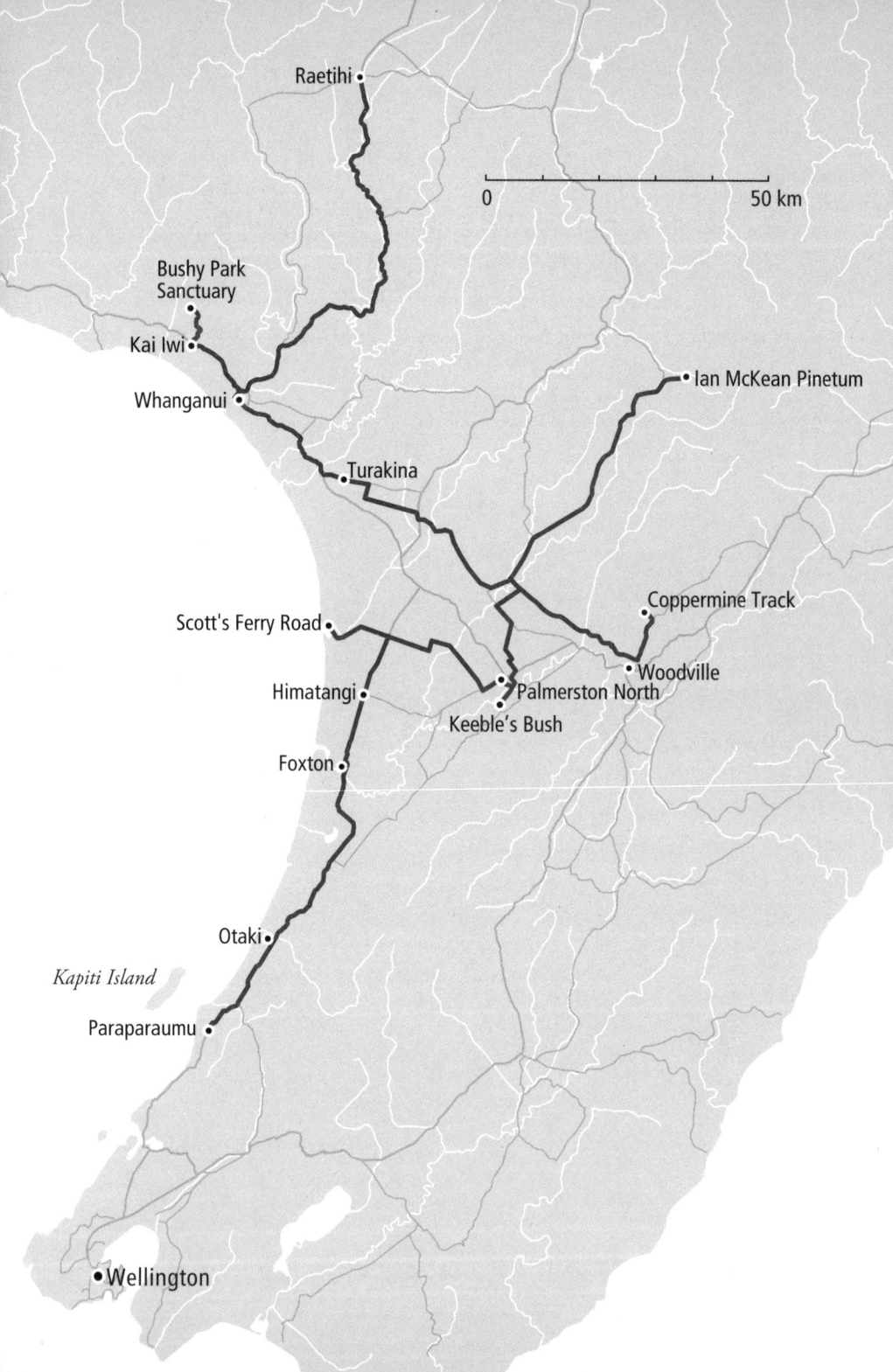

CHAPTER 5

Whanganui and Manawatu

This region stretches from around Patea in the north to near Paekakariki in the south and is bordered along its eastern limits by forests and forested ranges. It is dominated by three large rivers: the Rangitikei, the Manawatu and the Whanganui.

These rivers, and their riverine valleys and swampy hinterlands, were of major importance to local Iwi because of their rich resources and for the role they played in myth and tradition.

The area was heavily populated when Pakeha arrived. In 1843, the missionary Richard Taylor counted over a hundred canoes beached for one hui, along a remote upper tributary of the Whanganui.

But with Pakeha arrived much more lethal forms of warfare than Maori had previously known. Huge areas of land were soon depopulated by gun-toting taua, or war parties. But if the warfare was disastrous then the diseases that arrived with the Pakeha were catastrophic.

Evidence of once widespread settlement can still be seen in places. One example is the karaka groves, planted for their berries, still growing beside the 200 or so rapids along the navigable length of the Whanganui.

The Whanganui River is the second longest river in the North Island (after the Waikato River) and the main highway through the Whanganui National Park. It rises in the Matemateaonga Range to the west of Mt Tongariro, and follows a south-westerly curve for some 290 km before reaching the Tasman Sea at Whanganui City.

Allowing easy access to the central North Island, it was of great importance to the original people of the river, the Te Atihau Nui a Papa Rangi. The missionaries were quick to capitalise on this and they built many mission stations along the river, often with Maori names translated directly from

European names – Hiruharama (Jerusalem), Ranana (London), Koriniti (Corinth) and Atene (Athens).

Today stands of exotic trees such as poplars and willows, together with a few lonely gravestones, feral geese (kuihi) and rock pigeons (kuku) are often all that remain of most of these settlements. The poet James K. Baxter established a commune at Jerusalem and is now buried behind the church there.

Considerable numbers of native birds live along the river. A patient observer can almost always see tui, kereru, bellbirds, pied tits, robins and occasionally whiteheads. At night, too, around areas such as Whakahoro and Retaruke you are almost sure to hear moreporks. Listen for kiwi as well.

There have been a number of reports of piopio surviving in the bush backing onto Retaruke so keep a good look out – you would make ornithological history if you found one.

Native bats are also sometimes to be seen here and among the more interesting exotics along the Whanganui are feral peafowl (pikao) and guinea fowl. Look for them in scrubby areas or along the edges of the forest and particularly along the Tokomaru East River.

The completion of the main trunk railway early last century opened the region to settlers, who cleared the forest in the catchment area of the river. This led to heavy flooding, with rises in the river level of up to 20 m being recorded in the narrow gorges. The Whanganui River sustained further damage from the headwaters being diverted into the Tongariro Power Scheme in 1972. At times the river level has dropped so far that it has been difficult to navigate by boat. Fish and eels have died when the waters disappeared or the temperatures rose, and birds have left to find their homes in waters elsewhere. Along the main river the blue duck has had much of its habitat destroyed and is now very rare.

One of the Whanganui's major tributaries, the Manganui-o-te-Ao, has a brighter outlook. Along with the Motu on the East Coast, this river supports one of the few viable populations of blue duck in the North Island. However, the Manganui-o-te-Ao is a popular river with whitewater rafters and it was found that the duck was being unduly disturbed during its nesting season.

Fortunately, DoC officials and rafting companies are now cooperating to minimise the disturbance to the birds.

The headwaters of the Whanganui together with parts of the surrounding forest were gazetted as a national park in November 1986 and it is hoped that some of the fine stands of forest nearby, particularly those in Taranaki, might eventually be added to the park as well.

To explore the area, take SH4 from Whanganui inland and, shortly after reaching Upokongaro, about 14 km from the city, take the road off to the left along the river. This is a beautiful drive and follows the river a further 64 km, through Koriniti, Ranana and Jerusalem, as far as Pipiriki. Here the road turns east to Raetihi where you can take the main highways north or south or return to Whanganui along SH4. The round trip offers as wide a range of scenery as you could find anywhere in the North Island. Along the lower reaches of the river look out for the beautiful Nankeen night heron as this is, so far, our only breeding colony of this bird. It is however, nocturnal and very shy, but locals may be able to direct you to the roosting sites which you should watch from a distance.

The city of Whanganui lies at the junction of State Highways 3 and 4, on the flats near the mouth of the Whanganui River. The city services the surrounding rural area which is devoted mainly to sheep farming, but also to cattle, dairy and poultry farming.

Lake Virginia Reserve is the garden city's major attraction and lies west of the river, 3 km from the city centre. Lake Virginia was called Rotokawau by the locals for the number of little black and little shags to be found around it. I have seen both little black and little shags here and I'm told other species sometimes visit. Mute and black swans are both resident together with various ducks and other waterfowl/puwaiwai.

By following the west bank of the river towards the mouth you are almost sure to spot shags, dotterels, oystercatchers and godwits, as well as all three types of gull. Less common are royal spoonbills. Out at sea from the mouth are gannets, shearwaters and sometimes giant petrels. The Arctic skua is also a frequent visitor.

Bushy Park/Tarapuruhi, 8 km from Kai Iwi on the Whanganui-New Plymouth Highway has probably the finest area of native forest left in the Whanganui Region which includes rata, rimu, mahoe and pukatea along with some lovely tree ferns but the pride of the collection is a massive northern rata called, naturally enough, 'Ratanui' and which is about 1,000 years old. All of the original bush has been preserved, so take a few hours to wander around and enjoy a prime piece of subtropical rainforest. North Island robin (toutouwai), tieke and hihi (stitchbird) have all been reintroduced to Bushy Park and the robins and tieke have done so well that some have now been sent elsewhere. Bushy Park is an important kiwi creche.

This broad strip of land along the coast has been intensively farmed for well over a century and much of the rugged backcountry is under beef cattle and sheep. Consequently, most of the forest has disappeared with major stands being found now mainly along the Whanganui River and such places as the Waitotara Valley.

In this area north of Whanganui a number of important fossils have been found, notably around Kai Iwi. The first bones of the extinct North Island goose were found in a local swamp in 1886, together with a large number of moa bones which are now in the Whanganui Museum. Another interesting fossil found near Kai Iwi was an intact moa egg – unbroken specimens being very rare. This was found in a cave exposed by a roadside cutting and is also now in the local museum.

Travelling south from Whanganui along SH3 one crosses a number of rivers – the Whangaehu, Turakina and then the Rangitikei in Manawatu, and the last two are worth noting for the flocks of white cockatoos found along their headwaters. Just past Turakina, 21 km south-east of Whanganui, the Turakina Valley Road will take you to McPherson's Bush, a reserve with a number of native and exotic birds.

The Manawatu region is bounded in the east by the Ruahine and Tararua ranges, whose rugged terrain stands in marked contrast to the plains which lie between them and the Tasman Sea. The Manawatu River, for which the Manawatu area is named, rises in the eastern slopes of the Ruahines behind

Norsewood, before turning south and flowing through the Manawatu Gorge, which divides the Ruahines from the Tararuas. From this impressive gorge, gouged from the greywacke ranges, the river then flows out onto the largest plains in the North Island.

Away from the forested ranges the Manawatu is extensively farmed, predominantly in dairy herds. The lowlands once boasted extensive flax swamps which supported a flourishing fibre industry at Foxton, but in the 1950s the swamps were drained and have now been put into pasture.

Despite the widespread clearance of forest that has taken place since Pakeha settlement began, patches of bush still remain. Keebles Bush, 1.5 km south-west of Massey University in Palmerston North, has one of the best collections of native trees in the Manawatu. At 15 ha it is too small to support many native birds, although the exotics seem to like it.

Another tree collection worth seeing is the McKean Pinetum at Rangiwahia, 24 km north of Kimbolton. It is not quite as good as the tree collection at Eastwoodhill in Gisborne, but worth visiting for people used to seeing pine trees in state forests.

While native forests have always loomed large in the New Zealand consciousness it is only recently that an awareness of the worth of wetlands, tussocklands, shrublands and dunelands has grown. Suddenly people are discovering what makes their districts distinctive – whether a mangrove swamp, sand dunes covered with native plants, tussock grasslands or isolated fragments of bush hitherto ignored.

The dunelands of the Manawatu are certainly distinctive and some of the most representative of these can be reached via Scotts Ferry, about 19 km south-west of Bulls. These dunes are among the most exacting environments to be found anywhere in this country, with desiccating winds and temperatures, drifting sands, and low nutrient levels.

In response to duneland conditions a small group of highly specialised plants has evolved, of which pingao, an endemic sedge, and spinifex, a grass, are the most widespread. Spinifex is found on most beaches in the North Island and in the top half of the South Island, while pingao extends from

North Cape to Stewart Island and the Chathams. Pingao's graceful orange-green leaves make it one of the dunelands' most colourful plants and it was much used by Maori for weaving.

Despite its range, pingao is now under threat from the planting of exotic plants such as marram grass and tree lupin, both of which consolidate sand and destroy the shifting sands pingao favours. Other duneland plants are less common and some of them are becoming scarce. Among these are the shore milkweed, the sand daphne and two *Ranunculi*.

Any developed areas of the dune country are home to a surprisingly wide range of fauna, both native and exotic. Even the kereru relishes the protein-rich leaves of the nitrogen-fixing legumes. Swamps, lakes, scrub and open pastureland are all found here, along with sizeable stands of trees, and each of these habitats supports its own particular communities. Exotic birds flourish as do, sadly, their enemies the mustelids: rats, stoats and weasels.

In the winter, great flocks of finches inhabit the dunelands and feast on seeds. It is not altogether surprising that the decline of the kakariki and the extinction of the native quail (koreke) was accelerated by the introduction of these birds and their competition for food. The native insect-eaters are doing better against the foreign competition with large populations of warblers, fantails, kingfishers, pipits and even fernbirds to be seen.

Waterbirds are in their element in the chain of lakes and ponds in the hinterland of the dunes. Dabchicks and a wide range of ducks, including the scarce grey teal (tete moroiti) can be found, together with herons, rails and a number of waders. Brown teal (pateke) were once found here as well but have now disappeared, possibly because their habit of walking from the ponds or streams to their nesting sites left clear tracks for predators to follow.

The birds found in these wetlands now are, however, but a sad remnant of the avian population resident here until historical times. Many birds disappeared after the arrival of Maori and more still were harried into extinction by Pakeha. Introduced vermin, avian diseases and, most shamefully of all, the efforts of bird collectors each contributed to their demise.

Although all the rarer species were under pressure from collectors during the 19th century it was the huia, because of its beauty, that was singled out for special attention. J.G. Myers, writing in the *New Zealand Journal of Science and Technology* in 1923, blamed the decline in huia numbers on collectors.

But it was the demand for its striking feathers created by the royal visit of 1901 which sealed the huia's fate.

One influential figure of this period who had been alarmed at the rate at which the huia was declining was the then governor-general, the Earl of Onslow; the Earl tried to provide legal protection for the huia and several other species of birds. Indeed, he was sufficiently sympathetic to name his son 'Huia' when such names were definitely not *comme il faut*. He met the Maori chiefs of the Manawatu and Wairarapa districts at Otaki in 1891 and at this meeting one chief made the appeal: 'There, yonder, is the snow-clad Ruahine Range, the home of our favourite bird. We ask you, O Governor, to restrain the Pakehas from shooting it, that when your boy grows up he may see the beautiful bird that bears his name.'

Though the loss of any bird is tragic, that of the huia is especially sad. Besides the beauty of its plumage, it was the only known bird in the world where the beaks of the male and female differed, and dramatically so – the female beak was long and curved while that of the male was short and thick. It seems this difference served feeding functions, the male ripping off bark and the female probing the rotten wood exposed for grubs.

South towards Wellington through Foxton, Levin and Otaki the plain becomes gradually narrower, until after Paraparaumu the road is forced to follow a thin strip between the hills and the sea.

Foxton is worth visiting for the large numbers of birds which frequent the Manawatu estuary nearby. Each year black swans migrate north to the estuary from Lake Ellesmere in Canterbury, along with royal spoonbills and white herons from Marlborough and Westland. Cattle egrets and glossy ibises are infrequently seen here, as well as at nearby Lake Horowhenua.

In 1934, a Mediterranean shearwater was found dead on the beach at Foxton, 20,000 km from its nesting ground in the Atlantic. This undoubtedly earns this particular bird the title of the greatest avian aviator ever to be found in New Zealand.

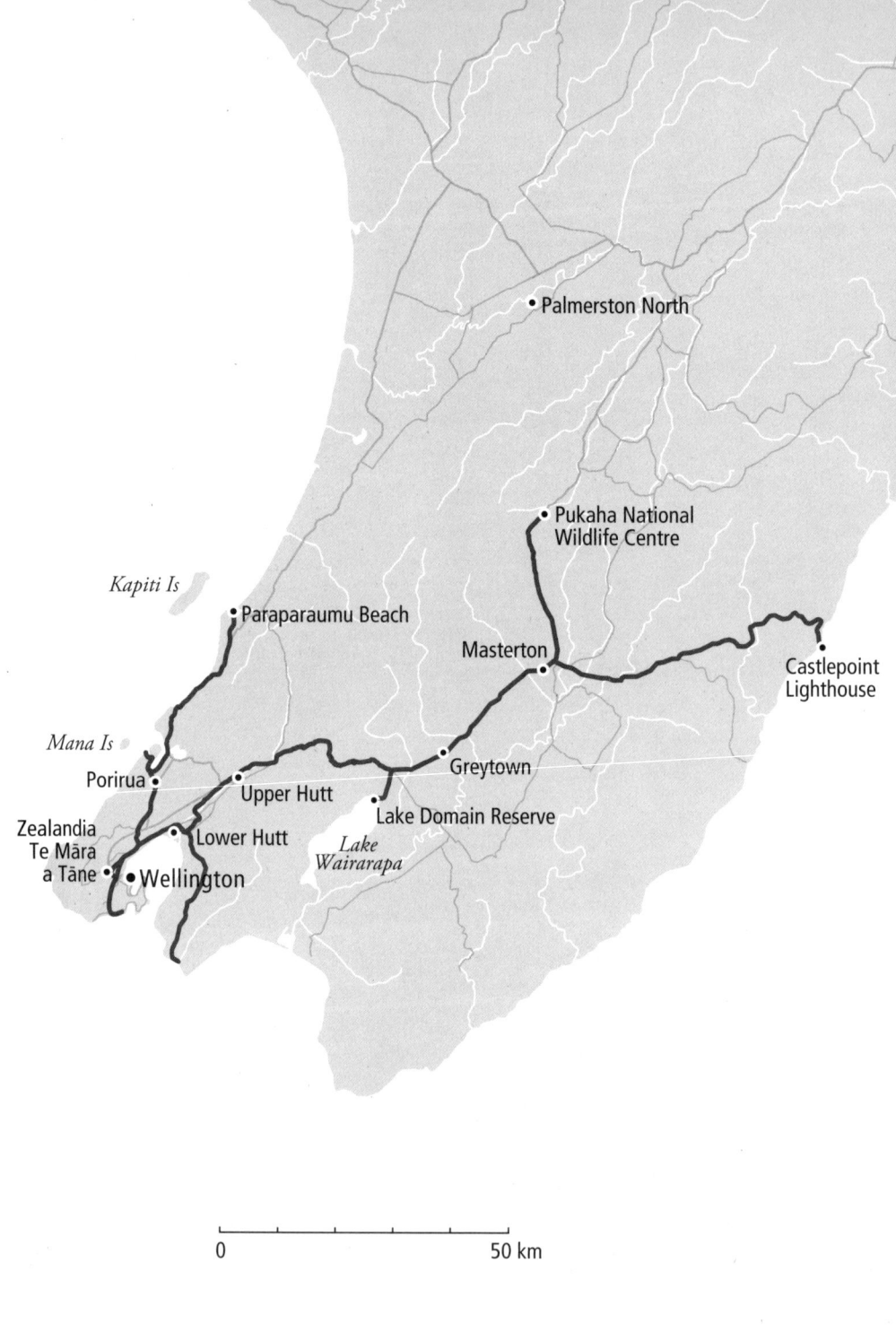

CHAPTER 6

Wellington/Te Whanganui a Tara and Wairarapa

The coastal drive into Wellington on SH1 is undoubtedly the most spectacular approach to any major city in New Zealand. The cliffs and hills plunge steeply to the sea and except on the calmest days are relentlessly pounded by waves and buffeted by the prevailing north-westerly winds. Along the coast between the Manawatu and Wellington the vegetation shows the effects of the salt-laden wind, and most exposed trees and shrubs are stunted and misshapen, clinging in tiny strips and patches to the hills. Exotic trees such as macrocarpa dominate the scenery and the land birds are almost all introduced species, which is hardly surprising since Wellington Harbour was a main port for importing livestock and birds.

Clearly visible from almost any part of the coastal road is Kapiti Island, some 10 km long and about 2 km wide and one of our most important island reserves. Kapiti was once partly farmed so the original vegetation has been severely modified. It also had a very large population of possums which killed some trees and badly damaged others.

Between 1918 and 1968 more than 25,000 possums were exterminated on Kapiti and in a concerted effort between 1980 and 1982 commercial trappers removed a further 15,000. Continuing eradication programmes eventually eliminated the few remaining.

The little spotted kiwi was introduced to Kapiti early last century and this is its last stronghold – none have been seen on the mainland for over 100 years. The rare South Island brown kiwi is also found here, and kokako, tieke and hihi have all been introduced in recent years.

A number of seabirds breed on Kapiti, among them the southern fairy prion and the titi, or sooty shearwater, and other seabirds frequently visit the waters around the island. The first recorded sighting of a grey-headed mollymawk (toroa) in our waters was made near Kapiti and rare visitors such as the thin-billed prion turn up occasionally.

Several wildlife luminaries have visited Kapiti, including the writer Gerald Durrell, who described his impressions in his book *Two in the Bush*. One of his more delightful descriptions is of a tui:

> *...a tui arrived, and it was quite obvious from the start that here was an artist down to the wingtips. He appeared suddenly in some bushes, casual and elegant, dressed in metallic green plumage picked out here and there with a purplish sheen. Overlying the greenish feathers on the back of his neck were fine, long, hair-like feathers in white, and at his throat he wore two small powder-puffs of white feathers that looked so exquisitely tied that even Beau Brummel might have envied it. The tui is about the size of a blackbird, but whereas the blackbird is plump and rather uncouth, the tui is slender and debonair and moves with all the ease and grace of a professional dancer.*

Kapiti lies close to a major migration route for whales moving through Cook Strait and because of this the island once had a shore-based whaling station. These migrations now mean that the beaches opposite the island are a 'hotspot' for whale strandings. Most of the recorded strandings of the common dolphin have been in this area and the largest stranding of orcas (kera wera), a pod of 17, came ashore at Paraparaumu in 1955. Other whales have beached here too, some of them cetacean rarities – Cuvier's beaked whales, straptooth whales and minke whales.

South along the coast there is a rather unusual reserve, at Pukerua Bay, 35 km north-east of Wellington. Created in 1985 for the protection of lizards, this 8 ha reserve is one of our smallest. On the steep hillside in the scrub and scree live five species of lizards, including the very rare Whitaker's skink, *Oligosoma whitakeri*, a nocturnal species so far found only in Pukerua Bay and on two small islands off the Coromandel Peninsula.

Because our lizards are generally small and inconspicuous many people are astonished to find how many species we have. Early scientists often failed to distinguish between similar species and, instead of the 39 lizard species once believed to be here there are actually around 120 and more are bound to be found particularly in alpine areas. Except for the 'kawekaweau' of the totara forests, lizards have, by a great deal of good luck, managed to escape extinction. But there is certainly no room for complacency, as many are now restricted to small islands where they are susceptible to calamities such as fires or the arrival of rats.

Just outside Porirua Harbour is the small island of Mana. Here the country's first commercial farm was established by John Bell, a Scot from Dundee, who landed in 1883, along with 10 cattle and 102 sheep. His farm flourished and only a year later the *Sydney Morning Herald* was able to announce that Mana was 'a very convenient place to refresh at... The anchorage is safe at all times, wood and water are both good and plentiful, and fresh beef, mutton, lamb and pork, with rabbits, poultry and vegetables, may be procured at Mr Bell's establishment on reasonable terms.'

Mana later became a quarantine station and new breeds of sheep were imported in the hope of establishing them in New Zealand. Unfortunately, an outbreak of disease meant that the stock had to be destroyed and the project abandoned. Now Mana is being turned into a reserve for rare and endangered species. Although after years of grazing only a small area remains in bush, it is hoped that it will eventually cover Mana again.

Five threatened species are found on Mana: McGregor's skink, the gold-striped gecko, the giant weta, a fern – *Anogramma leptophylla* – and Cook's scurvy grass. Other endangered animals will be introduced when the amount of vegetation permits. A number of species of birds and lizards have been reintroduced to the island, the most obvious of which is the takahe which are now breeding. Rowi, the rare southern kiwi, have been introduced to Mana and have been recorded breeding since 2016.

Another wildlife reserve that warrants a visit is at Pauatahanui. At the eastern extremity of the eastern arm of Porirua Harbour, this reserve is on ground that has been reclaimed but not in the usual manner. A disused cricket ground, a go-kart track and areas formerly grazed by stock are being allowed to revert to prime wetlands. Many new birds are now residents or regular visitors – mostly waders or waterbirds.

After Porirua Harbour SH1 runs inland through a low range of hills to Wellington and its spectacular harbour. Looking at the high-rises and houses of Wellington covering every piece of land that can be built on and the second growth, pine and gorse covering every bit that can't, it is difficult to imagine all this land forested. But more than a century ago birds abounded and even the huia was to be found inhabiting the steep valley of the Kaiwharawhara Stream, a kilometre from Wellington's present Central Post Office.

Once Pakeha settlement started, however, the onslaught on the forest and its inhabitants was swift and brutal. 'If it moves shoot it, if it doesn't chop it down!' seems to have been the slogan of the time. Singled out for particular attention were birds wanted by collectors, like the huia, or those wanted for the pot like the kereru and kaka.

The huia was under immense pressure, and as early as 1875 its slaughter in the Wellington area was worrying some people. In that year J. D. Eyns wrote:

> *The slaughter that came under my notice last year was so large, that I fear, when the country is more opened up, the poor huia will become extinct, a fate I shall much deplore, as anyone who has seen this most graceful bird alive can only regret that he has not oftener a chance of doing so. I am glad to say, one inducement to its destruction is wanting, as it is reported by all who have cooked it, to be a tough morsel.*

The gastronomic appeal of birds was important. William Delisle Hay, in his intriguing and quite extraordinary book, *Brighter Britain*, published in 1882, gave the following culinary ratings: tui are 'good eating', kuku or kereru are 'capital eating', weka 'eat like grouse', and the pukeko was 'fine eating'. About the only bird that Hay turned his nose up at was the kiwi which he considered indigestible:

> *Having eaten kiwi old and young, baked and boiled, roast and fried, I am able to state that its meat is tougher and more tasteless than barbecued boot soles...[i]f, as the naturalists lead us to infer, the moa*

was but a magnified kiwi in all respects, it is to be supposed that its flesh would be correspondingly tougher and coarser.

Pakeha settlement in the Wellington area took place some time after it began in the north and so exotic trees are not quite so well established. In addition they have had a more invigorating climate to contend with, the wind being responsible for the trees growing at such picturesque angles in the coastal areas. Despite being south of its natural range the pohutukawa does well here, with several fine specimens to be found around Wellington and in the Hutt Valley.

In the first flush of enthusiasm following settlement, hundreds of birds from sparrows (tiu) to blackbirds (manu pango) were also imported and liberated. A more recent arrival, and perhaps the most beautiful of all our exotic birds, is found in the foothills of Wellington. This is the crimson rosella, besides which its northern relative the eastern rosella seems positively pallid. Descended from cage birds which escaped in 1963, it is now seen in pairs or small family groups, occasionally straying north to the Taruruas and other areas.

The silvereye (tauhou) arrived in the North Island near Wellington in 1856 only to disappear after a few months. However, it returned with a vengeance in 1858 and has been here ever since. Maori, acknowledging it as a new arrival, called it tauhou, meaning stranger, and it is probably the only wild bird apart from the welcome swallow (warou) to arrive after Pakeha and earn itself a Maori name.

As in Auckland, there is plenty to see and do in Wellington for those with the time and transport. From Island Bay there is a nice walk around the beach to Red Rocks where fur seals haul out. They are not easy to see but their odoriferous fishy aroma gives them away.

When Pakeha arrived whales were found here in good numbers. In the 1840s there were a number of letters to the local newspaper complaining of the noise that right whales were making while cavorting in Port Nicholson, the Pakeha name given to Wellington Harbour. Apparently it was the mating season.

Before leaving Wellington, make a visit to Otari-Wilton's Bush in Wilton Road, Wilton, as this provides an excellent opportunity to study native plants in a confined area. One section of the reserve includes a good stand of native bush with kahikatea, rimu and rata. Another has a wide range of plants from coastal, montane and alpine regions, all labelled for easy identification. Native birds present include tui, fantail and silvereyes.

Another fine collection can be found in the Wellington Botanical Gardens. Here, in 25 ha of Central Wellington, are many exotic plants and trees together with a good selection of natives. It makes for pleasant strolling in fine weather and is best reached by taking the Kelburn cable car to the signposted stop and walking down to the Glenmore Street entrance. The Akapukaea, *Tecomanthe speciosa* climbing over the office building is superb.

When in Wellington, take the time to visit Zealandia. In the centre of Wellington over 200 ha of forest, wetlands and ponds have been enclosed by a predator-proof fence allowing the native avifauna to flourish and these have now been joined by quite a few other endemic species.

Kaka, in particular, have benefited from the protection afforded by the sanctuary and increasing numbers visit the suburbs and quite often help themselves to fruit from the residents' orchards. Little spotted kiwi and tuatara are among the fauna to be seen here.

Wellington also has many good walks. The Cannon Point Walk, on the outskirts of Upper Hutt, runs along the western edge of the Hutt Valley above Totara Park, which as the name indicates supports some large totara trees. Cannon Point itself is named for the remains of a large tree which resembled a cannon from a distance. Other vegetation includes such attractive subalpine species as the eyebright (tutae-kiore).

Another pleasing walk originates from Makara Beach on the west coast, 16 km from the city. Makara has long been popular with Wellingtonians and as early as 1865 they were pressing authorities to construct a road through the area 'to open up a source of recreation and pleasure... through some of the finest scenery in the province.'

This coast gets the full blast of Wellington's famous winds, resulting in

vegetation largely composed of low-lying, ground-hugging plants typified by such rugged species as pohue, mikimiki and tauhinu. The tussock grass *Poa caespitosa* and two normally alpine plants, the Spaniard and *Raoulia hookeri* with its silver-grey mats, can also be seen here.

Baring Heads, which is reached by the road which runs through Wainuiomata township and thence along the Wainuiomata River, is another pleasant excursion from the capital. Fur seals sometimes haul themselves out onto the rocks here and on fine days seabirds are often to be seen harrying the schools of fish offshore, activity which always brings to my mind James K. Baxter's verse:

Where spring seabirds mingle
Between the wave and sky,
The ka'wai chase the herrings in
Like soldiers dressed to die...

From Wellington SH2 continue north-east, climbing the Remutaka Ranges (spelt Rimutaka before 2017). Here, the first and probably the only examples of the bush wren or matuhi were taken in about 1850 by Captain Stolkes of the survey ship *Acheron*. They disappeared soon afterwards, apparently because of rat predation. The black petrel or taiko along with other petrels once nested in the Remutakas, but they have also been driven out by predators. Before the Pakeha arrived these hills supported dense forests filled with birdlife. Now all they support is scrub. For the best wildlife viewing in this area today you need to pass over the range and turn off at Featherston through Pigeon Bush – now with no pigeons and little bush – and travel to Lake Wairarapa.

There are several roads giving access to the lake but probably the most convenient approach is to take SH53 from Featherston towards Martinborough. A few kilometres from the town take Murphy Road which runs off to the right on to Domain Road and left to the Lake Reserve.

At 7,800 ha Lake Wairarapa is one of the largest lakes in the North Island and is surrounded by considerable areas of swamp. These wetlands support a great number of birds – 80 species have been recorded here – and it is a waterfowl habitat of international importance.

Lake Wairarapa drains into the smaller Lake Onoke, which is separated from the Pacific by a bar of shingle at the top of Palliser Bay. The bay itself, once densely settled by Maori, has been the site of extensive archaeological work which has given us some idea as to how the first New Zealanders lived. Old pa sites have been examined and middens excavated. From the remains of fish found in middens we know that species such as parrotfish and blue cod formed a large part of the diet of the early inhabitants over 600 years ago.

This area is also of interest to botanists. One of our rarer grasses, *Rytidosperma petrosum*, is found at Cape Palliser. Not described until 1979, this plant has so far only been found here and on D'Urville Island and Kapiti Island.

From Featherston, SH2 takes you north through the intensively farmed lands of the southern Wairarapa to Masterton, which can be used as a base for exploring this region.

To the west of Masterton rise the rugged, bush-clad Tararua Ranges and these serve as a poignant reminder of the former glory of the Wairarapa. It was from here that Buller took the only extant examples of the North Island laughing owl and the North Island kakapo. This Tararua forest, and a few sad remnants elsewhere, are all that now remain of the Forty Mile Bush which once extended from Mauriceville to Woodville and on to Dannevirke. In the 1850s, the missionary-explorer William Colenso talked of 'the dense nature of these almost impenetrable forests'. Alas, this is no longer so. More than a century of relentless clearance for farming by British and Scandinavian settlers, together with the operations of some 28 sawmills felling the many rimu, totara and matai, have changed the landscape forever.

A drive out to Castlepoint on the coast is worthwhile travelling via Blairlogie and Tinui. Castlepoint is the only settlement of any size along the entire length of coast between Cape Palliser and Cape Kidnappers. This is an area of great natural beauty with golden beaches, wild surf and striking headlands. Cook himself named Castlepoint for its fancied resemblance to the crenellated castles of Europe, but erosion has worked its inevitable course and today it bears little resemblance to what Cook saw.

Castlepoint has a number of points to interest the naturalist. Firstly, it is home to a very rare plant; the daisy, *Senecio compactus*, is found only here in a small, signposted reserve. Unlike a number of our plant rarities, which are modest in appearance, this is an attractive plant with thick grey-green leaves and large yellow flowers which would grace any garden.

The coast also supports a rich variety of seabirds, and even a great frigatebird has been collected at Castlepoint. Fur seals occur at various places, and the occasional sea elephant and sea leopard have turned up. If you find either of these animals treat them with a great deal of respect as they are fairly fractious.

North of Masterton the land is more open. Fine stands of poplars and oaks and glades of other exotic trees grace the landscape. The paddocks are dotted with grazing dairy herds of Friesians, Jerseys and occasionally Ayreshires; flocks of Romney and Southdown sheep flourish in the lush Wairarapa pastures.

The birdlife too is generally exotic. Mynas, which are at about their southern limit, test their luck with the oncoming traffic. Starlings, harriers and sparrows forage along the roadside verges and from the adjoining fields mixed flocks of finches flit overhead. Stop anywhere along the way and you are likely to hear the melodious flute-like call of the white-backed magpie, an Australian bird now well established in this area. Its beautiful call is one of the most evocative sounds of this part of the countryside. The poet Denis Glover described it as 'Quardle oodle ardle wardle doodle', which is probably as close as anyone could get to it and its call is about the only atractive thing about it.

Some 28 km north of Masterton, along SH2, is the Pukaha National Wildlife Centre at Mt Bruce. In a beautiful setting of native forest one can see the finest collection of New Zealand native birds to be found anywhere. Previously known as the Mt Bruce Native Bird Reserve, the centre was started by the former Wildlife Branch on the farm of Elwin Welch, a Wairarapa aviculturist, to propagate the takahe after its rediscovery in 1948. Later the centre was expanded to house and breed other endangered birds. In this, the centre has had some spectacular successes. Takahe, black stilts, North Island kokako, blue ducks, the North Island saddleback and both the brown and the little spotted kiwi are among the many birds to have bred here and some of these are now second- or third-generation breeders. Wander past the many enclosures dotted throughout the beautiful native bush reserve and you will see and hear species like the shore plover and Forbes parakeet, which are kept nowhere else. Take your time – the aviaries are very well planted so only by careful observation will you see some of our more secretive bird species.

Watch for the birdlife in the surrounding bush as well. Many smaller native birds such as fantails and whiteheads are found at Mt Bruce in reasonable numbers and by rigorously keeping the possum population in check the centre has enabled the surrounding forest to regenerate to something like its former state. Besides birds, the centre also houses tuatara, various lizards and native bats in its nocturnal house. Also watch out for the enormous eels and trout which loiter under the bridges, waiting for handouts.

The takahe, however, remains the highlight of the collection and from the centre's coffee shop there is a fine view of a breeding pair in an adjoining enclosure. It is the most colourful of all New Zealand's birds, as well as being among the rarest. The North Island takahe once occurred naturally in the Wairarapa – possibly as recently as the 19th century.

From Mt Bruce, SH2 continues on to Hawke's Bay through Eketahuna, Pahiatua, Woodville and Dannevirke. Virtually all of this country is now in farmland, where once it was forest, and birds abounded. Piopio, whekau, huia and kakapo were all present then, together with the kokako, which early Pakeha settlers called 'blue-gills'. These have now all disappeared and even the small pockets of bush that still remain are eerily empty of sound.

CHAPTER 7

Hawke's Bay/Te Matau a Maui

Hawke's Bay is essentially a fertile but not very extensive plain – the Heretaunga Plain – backed by rolling uplands rising up to the mountainous spine of the North Island. Only in a few places is there more than 60 km between the summits and the sea. The climate is temperate and equable and this, together with the low rainfall, makes Hawke's Bay the leading horticultural area of New Zealand.

The rolling foothills had mostly been cleared of trees by a series of fires when Pakeha arrived and aspiring pastoralists were quick to see the potential of this empty land. As the local farmer-naturalist Herbert Guthrie-Smith said, they then set to and it was 'stamped, jammed, hauled and murdered into grass.'

The widespread destruction of the forest meant that most birds in pre-European times probably lived along the rivers and seashore; apart from the now extinct native quail, or koreke, and the pipit there were few true grassland dwellers. This left an ecological gap that was rapidly filled by the introduced birds, and exotic mammals soon made themselves at home in what cover remained in the surrounding hills.

Mule deer imported from the United States were liberated in Hawke's Bay around 1909, but did not survive. However, red deer and sika are both found today, the red deer descended from animals brought from Otago and liberated on Matapiro Station in about 1910. From here they spread into the Kaimanawa Range, the Kaweka Range and the Urewera country, with some animals migrating as far away as Taupo.

Sheepfarming in Hawke's Bay started early. In 1848 Henry Tiffin and James Northwood drove 3,000 merinos up the coast to stock 20,000 hectares of land which had been leased from Maori at Pourerere and Omakere.

Driving so much stock through rugged country in those unsettled times was a considerable feat, which unfortunately has received little recognition.

On your way to Hawke's Bay, try to make a side trip to the Ruahine Forest Park which forms the watershed between the Manawatu and southern Hawke's Bay. The park can be reached by taking the Tamaki East and West Roads from near Dannevirke, or the Ngamoko Road from Norsewood. The park displays a variety of vegetation, supporting a range of birds both exotic and native. Red and sika deer are found here, together with pigs, hares and possums. Above 1,400 m there is alpine tussock which changes to subalpine scrub, then beech as one descends. This gives way to mixed podocarp-beech and podocarp at the lower levels, but in the north, parts of this forest have been destroyed by fire and replaced by scrub.

One of the things to watch for in Hawke's Bay is the area's fine exotic trees. There are some particularly good examples on some of the sheep stations, at Te Aute College 28 km south of Hastings on SH2, and also in the streets of Hastings and Napier. There is a well-established avenue of Norfolk pines along Napier's waterfront and this is brilliantly lit up with decorations at Christmas time. Frimley Park in Hastings has some particularly good tree specimens which include a splendid necklace poplar. In autumn a drive along Oak Avenue in Hastings is spectacular because of the blaze of colour provided by the 1600 m stretch of giant oak trees.

There are also some good stands of native trees but these take some seeking out. At Ball's Clearing, about 5 km west of Puketitiri, which is some 50 km north-west of Napier, there is one of the finest stands of podocarp forest remaining in New Zealand, and the native trees at A'Deanes Bush, west of Waipukurau in the foothills of the Ruahines, are particularly good with an especially fine totara.

To find the native bush birds, you must travel some way in from the coast. One place to start is in the Kaweka Forest Park to the west of Hawke's Bay, which can be reached by travelling along the Napier-Puketitiri Road north-west of Napier. This area was greatly modified by fires that once devastated Hawke's Bay and heavy native bush survives only in the sheltered valleys, the remainder of the park being made up of about equal parts of scrub and tussock in the north-east and beech-podocarp forest in the north.

Native birds that can still be found in the Kawekas include whio, kiwi and kakariki but an almost complete range of feral mammals is found there too – pigs, deer, rabbits, possums, hares, goats and even wild sheep. Many of the other birds that are of interest in Hawke's Bay are either exotics or self-introduced species called adventives. There are wild turkeys inland from Tutira Station together with feral peafowl at Waimarama. Although black swans have been in the Bay for some time the white species, called the mute swan, was until recently not present; in the last few years a young pair of the mute swan has, however, been liberated on Horseshoe Lake to try to establish the species here.

One of our most attractive recent immigrants, the black-fronted dotterel was first seen near Napier in 1954. It breeds in the Esk and Rangitikei riverbeds and from here it has spread throughout the lower part of the North Island and into Nelson and Marlborough where it has colonised other shingle riverbeds.

The best of Hawke's Bay's wildlife attractions is the gannet colony at Cape Kidnappers. Cook traded with local Maori for fish near the Cape in late 1769. While here he mentioned the gannets or 'Solander geese'; they provided his Christmas dinner, yet he made no note of their nesting here. About 100 years later when the naturalist Henry Hill visited the cape he found a colony of about 50 birds, which he estimated had been using the site for some 20 years. By about 1914, when the colony was made a reserve, nearly 2,300 birds were nesting and today there are probably around 20,000 gannets. This was the world's first mainland gannet colony, and for a long time the only one known, because gannets usually nest on small, rocky, offshore islands. Other mainland colonies have become established at Muriwai, north of Auckland, and at Farewell Spit in Nelson.

While here take some time to study the domestic arrangements of the gannets if you can. Each nest consists of a few twigs and bits of seaweed, scrapped together just out of range of the rapier-sharp beak of the next bird. Any minor miscalculation by a landing bird means running a gauntlet of the stabbing beaks of outraged neighbours to get home. One must wonder why they bother nesting in colonies when they get on so poorly with each other.

The accessibility of the colony has made it a prime study area for ornithologists. To get to Cape Kidnappers from Hastings drive to Clifton, which is 21 km from the city, and from here there is a 7 km walk along the beach. It is important to check the dates of opening and the tides before setting off. Access is sometimes restricted because of rockfalls. There are also 4WD excursions along the cliff-tops.

While you are in this area check out the Cape Kidnappers and Ocean Beach Wildlife Preserve. This was created by the building of a 10.6 km predator-proof fence across the Cape Kidnappers Peninsula in 2006, enclosing 2,500 ha and this was followed by a move to eradicate predators which was largely successful. Since then a number of birds have been introduced, including two species of kiwi -the eastern race of the North Island brown kiwi and the little spotted kiwi, and a variety of bush birds. The kiwi and the bush birds are almost all breeding and the two kiwi species are doing particularly well although they seem to prefer different habitats.

Also a number of seabird chicks have been moved to the sanctuary and it will be interesting to see how these fare. The founding juveniles were 200 grey-faced petrels (oi) and 250 Cook's petrels (titi) which were placed in burrows which had been dug for them, where they joined resident fluttering shearwaters (pakaha).

From Clifton the bay curves in a wide arc to Napier, and on the seashore around Napier are large numbers of adventive flowering plants. You get a particularly good view of these from the main highway just north of the city, where they tend to crowd out the less rugged native plants. The widespread planting of marram grass along this coastline to stabilise sand dunes has made much of this habitat unsuitable for breeding shorebirds and further threatened native plants.

A drive along the waterfront around Napier is always interesting. The National Aquarium of New Zealand on Marine Parade is probably the best in the country. Besides fish, they also have some good reptile exhibits but the main feature of the aquarium is a 400,000 litre tank in which many kinds of fish from Hawke Bay are found. NB The sea is called Hawke Bay while the land is Hawke's Bay.

Still further along Marine Parade is the nocturnal wildlife centre where kiwi and other nocturnal animals can be seen. A number of the kiwi exhibited here were bred at nearby Greenmeadows, which pioneered the propagation of kiwi in captivity.

On the slopes of Hospital Hill are the Napier Botanical Gardens. An unusual feature of the gardens is the large flock of free-flying budgies. They spend the day flying around the neighbourhood before returning each night to their cages. Unlike wild budgies in their native Australia, which are almost entirely green, these, because of selective breeding, display a variety of colours.

Napier is probably best known for the earthquake that devastated the town in 1931. One consequence was the raising of the bed of the harbour at Napier, which created an extensive area of salt marsh, providing an ideal habitat for waders. Five kilometres north of Napier beside SH2 is the Ahuriri Wildlife Refuge/Ahuriri Estuary and large numbers of migratory and shorebirds are found here. Kotuku are often seen in winter and godwits in the summer months. There is also a large number of ducks.

Continue along SH2 and the first major river that you reach from Napier is the Esk. From here it is an easy drive north to Tutira Station. One of our best-known amateur naturalists, Herbert Guthrie-Smith, purchased Tutira in 1882 and spent most of his adult life at the station. He wrote his classic works in the homestead on the rise across the road from Lake Tutira. These included his best-known work, *Tutira*, as well as several other very readable books on birdlife. The Arboretum and Education Centre on the site are named in his honour.

Guthrie-Smith was a pioneer of bird photography in New Zealand and, considering the limitations of his cumbersome and primitive equipment, the results were remarkable. He wrote:

> *I have commited crimes in my life, I know, Who hasn't? But I believe exiation may have been accomplished during those hours of anguish, kneeling on a waterproof and slowly sinking into the ooze.*

It was in such a position that he photographed several bird species now gone from Tutira, including the blue duck, weka, falcon and brown teal.

There are still, nevertheless, numerous waterfowl to be seen on and around the lake. The Australian coot first appeared in this country at Lake Tutira in 1954 and has since spread to many other parts of the country.

And a short distance from Tutira is Waitere. This relatively small – less than 2,000 ha – area of scrubland lies inland from Tutira towards the Mohaka River, off the Napier-Gisborne Highway. Today it is in the process of regenerating after a series of disastrous fires and is of note because it shelters the largest group of kiwi in Hawke's Bay – between 30 and 50 birds. These birds have disappeared from virtually every other area in Hawke's Bay because of the burning-off of their habitat and predation.

Also from Tutira a visit to the Boundary Stream Mainland Island is well worthwhile. Turn left at the Tutira Store and follow the Boundary Stream signposts. After six kilometres turn left into Pohokura Road and follow it to the Boundary Stream carpark and on the way you will pass the Lake Opouahi Kiwi Creche.

Boundary Stream Mainland Island extends over an 800 ha limestone landscape, which since pest control was started, is now home to a number of rare species including Kiwi, Kokako and the NZ Falcon (Karearea) along with all the usual bush birds. Also found here are a number of botanical rarities including the endangered Kakabeak (ngutu kaka) and the Yellow-flowered Mistletoe (pirita). Shine Falls, the highest falls in Hawke's Bay, is a pleasant walk past spectacular limestone formations and through prime forest.

After Tutira, following SH2 brings you to the Mohaka River. This has for a long time been a favourite with anglers but now it has another significant claim to fame. For many years, when people talked of fossils in New Zealand, they invariably meant only marine animals such as ammonites, as it was widely believed that because of our isolation land animals such as the dinosaurs had never reached these islands.

Then in the mid-1980s an amateur palaeontologist, Joan Wiffen, from Haumoana in Hawke's Bay, found an eight centimetre bone in a tributary of

Boat trips to the Poor Knights Islands from Tutukaka permit the sighting of many sea birds including rareities.

A North Island Saddleback/Tieke is commonly seen on Tirititi Matangi Island.

Thermal areas such as this have interesting residents called thermaphiles.

Rare birds such as Blue Duck/Whio, Kiwi and Kaka are in good numbers around Lake Waikaremoana.

A lot of work on conserving the flora and Fauna of Mt. Taranaki has been carried out and the walks are enchanting.

The tui is often seen throughout Aotearoa. particularly when trees like the kowhai are in flower.

This gannetry at Cape Kidnappers is the largest in the country.

The bird population at Zealandia Sanctuary is thriving and now often visits surrounding urban areas

French Pass/Anaru is where much of the early scientific research was carried out by English and French explorers.

Kaikoura is a top destination for birders and whale-watchers.

The Yellow-eyed Penguin/Hoiho is now the world's rarest penguin. Give it plenty of space.

Often called the Mt. Cook Lily by the locals, this is actually the world's largest buttercup.

Kea can usually be seen around the glaciers along with smaller bird species and interesting sub-alpine plants.

A wide range of alpine plants and animals, some quite rare, can be seen around the lakes in the Southern Alps.

Lake Okarito, which is really a lagoon, is home to a number of water birds, and has resident Kotuku.

Little Blue Penguins and Yellow-eyed Penguins are found in bush around the Moeraki Boulders.

The Weka on Ulva Island are very tame so keep an eye on your belongings.

the Te Hoe River, which flows into the Mohaka. Palaeontologists found that this tiny bone came from a medium-sized, two-legged, carnivorous dinosaur called a therapod. It was probably about seven metres long, stood about two metres tall, and weighed slightly less than half a tonne. After that Joan Wiffen found another dinosaur fossil, a pelvic bone from the bird-hipped hypsilophodon.

Moa enthusiast Bill Hartree has also located a number of the nesting sites of moa in the steep Hawke's Bay hill country and from the bones nearby he has been able to identify the birds as being *Anomalopteryx* spp. He concluded that the moa laid a single egg and the nest was usually sheltered by rock overhangs. Moa tracks were once to be seen along steep hillsides in several parts of the province, but erosion and stock movements have now largely destroyed these.

From the Mohaka River north, the country shows the serious erosion which is a feature of the east coast. This erosion has a number of causes but chief among these is overgrazing, and unplanned forest clearance. This erosion was greatly accelerated by damage caused by the earthquake of 1931 which was centred near Wairoa. A few small patches of forest remain, mostly along the rivers, and these support mixed companies of native and exotic birds.

From Wairoa itself there are two routes north to Gisborne: the coastal route along SH2 and the inland route via Frasertown and Tiniroto. At Frasertown there is a turn-off that will take you by way of SH38 to Lake Waikaremoana in the Te Urewera country and then eventually to Rotorua, a detour well worth making, but watch out for speeding drivers and wandering stock.

On the road to the lake, keep a lookout for Bobwhite quail which were introduced in 1894 and, although not establishing themselves elsewhere, survived here. For some reason they disappeared in the 1920s but were found again in 1952 to the south of the Waikaremoana Road. Superficially similar to the California quail, they differ by having no crest and have a different chest pattern.

Te Urewera is a protected area, and former national park, covering almost 200,000 ha. It is without doubt the finest area of natural bush remaining in the North Island and as it ranges from about 150 m to 1,400 m in altitude it encompasses a wide variety of vegetation. Also found here are Lakes Waikaremoana and Waikareiti, among the most beautiful lakes in the North Island.

This area gives a good idea of what New Zealand was like before humans arrived. From any high area, the vegetation stretches like a green undulating carpet into the distance. In the lower areas around the lakes the dominant trees are rata, rimu and tawa. As you move higher, the rata and tawa are gradually replaced by beech. Higher still, only beech is found. This, too, is found in successive altitudinal layers – first red beech, then silver beech and, at the highest reaches, the mountain beech.

Of particular interest to botanists is the presence at Lake Waikaremoana of the kakabeak shrub, the kowhai-ngutu-kaka of Maori. Curiously, although this plant is well known to the home gardener, in the wild it is a very rare plant indeed, limited to about a dozen plants growing near the lake, a few on Great Barrier Island, together with some in the inlets of the Bay of Islands and on the coast near Thames.

The fauna of the area is relatively diverse. Most evenings near the lake you will see the beautiful puriri moth which is often attracted by lights. You will certainly hear the plaintive cry of the morepork, and probably that of the kiwi. Shags, tui and kereru and many smaller birds can be spotted moving about the forest fringes. In the smaller streams whio can be seen, and grey ducks, mallards, paradise shelducks and scaup all frequent the lake.

The visitor centre provides comprehensive information about the flora and fauna of the area. While tramping through the bush around the lakes watch for some of the scarcer native birds. Kaka, kakariki, korimako, pied tits and robins are all to be found, but kokako seem to have disappeared from this particular area. Also some of the last sightings of the bush wren (matuhituhi) and piopio were from the Urewera. Of considerable interest too, was the sighting in 1924 by William Cobeldick, a ranger based in Rotorua, of a pair of huia in the bush near Lake Waikareiti, as well as a single huia at Taharua Stream near the source of the Mohaka River in the same year.

While living in the Urewera area between 1895 and 1910, Elsdon Best, one of Aotearoa's first ethnologists, asked the Tuhoe which birds had disappeared from their area and the list they gave him was as follows: whekau, or hakoke, the laughing owl; kakapo; kaha, the grebe; kareke, the marsh rail; koitareke, the quail; kotuku; mohopatatai, the land rail; kea; mohorangi; momotawai, the bush wren; tieke; and tihe, the stitchbird.

It is obvious that these names include a number of Tuhoe dialectal names, different from other Maori dialectal names for these birds (for example, mohopatatai for mohopereru, and koitareke for koreke).

However, the two I find particularly interesting are kea and mohorangi. The kea has not been reported elsewhere in the North Island and in the South Island it is a bird of the mountains, yet Best obviously was not confusing the Urewera 'kea' with kaka, as he describes the kea as being a smaller bird frequenting the open country and with a differently shaped bill. He also says it was *he manu ahua where* – 'of a brownish or reddish colour'.

The other mysterious name is mohorangi. "Rangi" has a variety of translations including day. Does that mean it was a diurnal rail? If so, we still don't know which rail it refers to and it may well have been the takahe.

Being an inland people far from the rich coastal food resources and separated from them by often hostile tribes, Tuhoe were entirely dependent on the forests for their food. Elaborate rituals often attended food-gathering, and ornate and well-manufactured utensils were used in the snaring of birds and for storing them. Best collected many of these and they are now in the Dominion Museum in Wellington.

Heading back towards Wairoa from Te Urewera takes you first to Frasertown, from which there are two routes north. The inland route will take you through more scenic country. It gives you the opportunity of seeing many bush birds and of visiting the tree collection at Kaikiore, near Tiniroto. This arboretum contains a very good collection of both native and exotic trees, many of which are quite rare specimens.

There are a number of native birds found here and these include the bellbird and the robin, both of which keep to the heavier bush. Magpies and harriers are common in the more open country, and Canada geese (kuihi), a recent introduction, are often to be seen in the more open areas, especially near farm ponds.

By comparison the coastal road to Gisborne brings you to the Mahia Peninsula, the main attraction of this locality. While here be sure to visit the Mahia Scenic Reserve. This is a small but beautiful oasis of coastal broadleaf-nikau forest which provides a stark contrast to its neighbouring landslide scarred East Coast hill country.

Mahia has a distinctive shape, rather like that of a giant fish hook, and this promontory curving out to sea and then back towards the land serves as a natural whale trap. The echolocation of the whales is confused by the unusual topography and by following the curve of the land they find themselves in shallow water and thus trapped.

It is significant that only the toothed whales which use echolocation have been trapped here. Sperm whales (paraoa) are regularly stranded along with the pygmy sperm whale (76 of the 114 recorded strandings of this species have been at Mahia). An unusual occurrence here has been the number of simultaneous strandings of two whale species. In 1962 seven false killer whales came ashore along with three pygmy sperm whales; four pygmy sperm whales and a pilot whale in 1972; and a pygmy sperm whale together with a beaked whale in 1980.

Only a few kilometres off Mahia Peninsula is Portland Island/Waikawa and this is where a colony of the prettiest of our shorebirds the shore plover (tuturuatu) is found, having been moved here from the Chathams/Rekohu via Mt Bruce. However the only hope for the long-term survival of this bird, is if Waikawa can be kept predator free.

Some 40 km north-east of Wairoa are the Morere Hot Springs. Although the springs are not all that marvellous, they are set in a 200 ha patch of bush which contains some very nice nikau palms – a small remnant of the extensive podocarp and mixed hardwood forests which once clothed the East Coast. Native birds including tui, kereru and korimako, are to be found here.

Continuing north the road takes you through a wide variety of habitats which in turn support a variety of wildlife. There are few extensive stands of forest but most of this was turned into farmland around the turn of the 19th century and a lot of it now seems to be working its way back to its original state. Bad erosion is apparent and where the soil cover has been stripped from the land, ugly blue-grey and yellow patches from the underlying mudstone show through.

From the hills near Muriwai, 36 km on from Morere, good views can be had over the alluvial flatland surrounding the Waipaoa River towards Gisborne across Poverty Bay, and this despite its name is one of the most productive regions in the country – the lush vineyards, orchards and market gardens offer a sharp contrast to the often ravished hill country around them.

CHAPTER 8

Poverty Bay/Turanganui-a-Kiwa, East Cape and Gisborne

Poverty Bay was settled centuries ago by Ngati-Porou and, when Cook arrived in October 1779, their settlements and pa were scattered over a large area of the East Coast. Cook's encounters with the locals were not happy ones and after a few days of trying to establish friendly relations with the Ngati-Porou, he set sail noting:

> ...we weighed anchor and left this unfortunate, inhospitable place, on which we bestow the name of Poverty Bay, as it did not afford a single article which we wanted, except a little firewood.

'Poverty' was a massive misnomer as the bay is now the centre of one of our most productive agricultural and horticultural areas. This development has not been without its cost however. Pioneer farmers, anxious to make their land productive, removed large areas of bush with disastrous consequences. The steeply sloping land, denuded of its cover, was unable to hold the soil after heavy rain and now shows the scars of enormous erosion.

Gisborne, the region's biggest city, is pleasantly sited where the Waimata and Taruheru Rivers join to form the Turanganui River and with more than 2,200 hours of sunshine annually has one of the country's best climates. The Botanical Gardens, adjoining the Taruheru River, off Roebuck and Aberdeen Roads, has some fine specimen trees and an aviary which includes weka, and there is a particularly nice Norfolk Island Pine on Haronga Road.

Outside the city an easy drive of some 35 km along the Rere Ngatapa Road brings you to the superb, exotic tree collection at Eastwoodhill Arboretum. Here, one can find the life's work of a local farmer, William Douglas Cook. Returning from service in Europe after the First World War, Cook decided to create a replica of the English stately gardens he had admired while overseas.

He spent his life's savings planting nearly half of his 130 ha farm in trees, almost all imported from the Northern Hemisphere, and today Eastwoodhill has the best collection of this type of tree in the country. Many of the trees growing at Eastwoodhill Arboretum are now rare in their native lands and seed has recently been re-exported to Britain. Eastwoodhill is regarded by arboricultutrists as the national arboretum.

Autumn is the time when the many deciduous trees are at their finest; in spring, the thousands of daffodils are in bloom and the magnolias and rhododendrons are in full flower. Rather surprisingly, the flowers do not seem to attract many of our native birds. There are a few tui here, together with kereru, riroriro and piwakawaka, but for the most part the birds, like the trees, are exotics.

It is definitely too big for a flying visit, so pack a picnic lunch and make a day of it.

On the way back to Gisborne keep a sharp lookout for weka, as this part of Poverty Bay was one of the few places in the North Island where this bold, brassy and inquisitive bird still occurred when it disappeared from the rest of the North Island.

Weka nests are built under logs or rock overhangs and often also around outbuildings, such as the maize cribs once a feature of the Gisborne area. Although flightless, the weka is among the best suited of our native birds to withstand the onslaught of introduced predators, making short work of rats, mice and, occasionally, even stoats and weasels. However, disease, presumed to have been spread by introduced poultry, was almost the wekas undoing. It disappeared from most of the country between 1916 and 1930, but fortunately small remnant populations survived both here and in Northland, and weka trapped locally have been used to replenish parts of their former range.

These transfers, however, have not always been to the wekas' liking. A bird captured from Gisborne and released in Hawke's Bay promptly walked the 130 km home and some South Island birds, after being liberated on Maud Island in the Marlborough Sounds, swam almost a kilometre back to the mainland. When camping in areas where weka are found, make sure that your goods and chattels are secure as weka, like kea, are no respecters of either possessions or privacy – a fact the early bushmen and explorers soon found out. I am still a little nonplussed as to what possible use a weka could have had for a rather expensive camera filter it souvenired from me one day when I was camped in this locality.

Lake Repongaere, 5 km north of Patutahi and only about 20 minutes drive from Gisborne, is a good place for viewing waterfowl or manuwai. At certain times of the year the lake is home to thousands of waterbirds, including grey ducks and paradise shelducks, black swans, mallards, shovelers and grey teal. And a remarkable phenomenon which occurs annually in many parts of New Zealand can be witnessed here. About a week before the shooting season starts, ducks and swans flock into sanctuaries and other protected waters.

From Gisborne there are two routes to the Bay of Plenty. The quickest is by way of Te Karaka, Matawai and the Waioweka Scenic Highway along SH2, but the more scenic way is via the East Cape on SH35.

To take the inland route, leave Gisborne and head towards Matawai. The road travels through vineyards, market gardens and dairy farms to Te Karaka. With its large orange berries and big, glossy leaves, the karaka is among the most distinctive of our trees. It was an important food for Maori and karaka groves often indicate former pa sites. The berries are poisonous without long and careful preparation; Maori would boil the berries several times, pouring away the water each time until the pulp was safe to eat.

The Matawai area is the demesne of the magpies (makapi), and both the white-backed and the black-backed forms now reign over virtually all of the cleared country, terrorising other bird species and, according to the locals, causing a decline in the numbers of tui and kereru found hereabouts. They even harry the harrier, the largest of our hawks, and it is now a common sight to see one fleeing from an irate pair of nesting magpies.

One of the few native birds that is flourishing between Te Karaka and Matawai and on into the Waioweka Gorge is the paradise shelduck (putangitangi). Many ponds for watering stock have been constructed in this area in recent years and virtually every one of these ponds now has a pair of resident paradise shelducks. This shelduck is one of the few birds in New Zealand that is sexually dimorphic – that is, with differing plumage for each sex. The most striking difference is that the head of the male is black with a greenish sheen, while that of the female is white. It gathers in large flocks in winter and congregations of many hundreds of ducks are commonly seen on recently harvested maize fields near Otoko, although many farmers consider them to be pests as they foul pastures.

Apart from the paradise shelducks, harrier hawks, fantails, kingfishers and the occasional pipit, almost all the birds you will find near Matawai are introduced species. Finches, blackbirds and thrushes abound and starlings are once again appearing as magpies rout their foe the myna, an enthusiastic competitor with the starling for nesting sites.

Near Wairata, the bush returns and with it the native birds. At this altitude of almost 800 m the typical rimu-rata-tawa bush of the lower altitudes gives way to the rimu-beech forests of the mountains. The birds here include such bush species as kereru, tui, korimako, tits, robins, falcons, whiteheads and riflemen which can all be found in this area, although the numbers of these last two species are now diminishing. Kaka still occur, but if you want to see or hear them it is best to heed the Maori proverb 'Kua taki te kaka' and be up early. This translates as "The kaka has called" and means that dawn has arrived.

The coastal route around the East Cape along SH35 passes the fine stand of Norfolk pines along Kaiti Beach, then goes through Wainui, Makarori and Puawa before turning inland. This is hilly country where Cook first glimpsed New Zealand, describing it thus: '... *the face of the country is of a hilly surface and appears to be clothed with wood and verdure*'. The 'wood and verdure' have long since gone and with them much of the protection from erosion these hills once enjoyed.

The forest in this region then consisted of mixed pohutukawa, karaka, puriri, kohekohe and nikau. Now few pockets of this coastal forest are left except in a narrow band along some coastal fringes, and in the open country almost all the trees that are to be seen are exotics.

The road reaches the sea again at Tolaga Bay and here a long wharf runs out into the bay from near the fine stand of conifers on the south side of the Bay. Although now disused, this wharf is quite safe and the 30 minute walk to its end sometimes enables you to see seabirds which are usually out of sight from the beach. Penguins are not uncommon, together with various petrels, mollymawks and gannets.

While Cook was at Tolaga Bay, Joseph Banks, the expedition scientist, collected some 20 species of trees and noted the presence of mulberry trees that Maori had brought with them from Hawaiki. These have now long gone. Cook traded with local Maori for kumara and also brewed local plants as antiscorbutic teas for his often unenthusiastic crew.

And then in July 1834, the Jewish trader Joel Polack sailed into Tolaga Bay to repair his cutter *Emma* which had been damaged sailing down from Thames. Here, Polack was presented with *'the petrification of the bones of large birds'* and thus the moa first came to the attention of Pakeha. Polack was told that the bones had come from the foot of Mt Hikurangi, from birds that had become extinct because of the ease of trapping them.

Polack's description of the bones was published on his return to England and these writings were later denounced in most unscientific terms by the botanist William Colenso, who labelled their discovery a fabrication. However, there is little reason to doubt Polack's account and Colenso's outburst can thus be regarded simply as professional and antisemitic pique.

In fact, the first moa fossil to be scientifically examined also came from the East Coast and was collected by a trader, John Williams Harris, who had a shore whaling station near the present site of Gisborne. This was only a fragment of a femur but it was sufficient for Sir Richard Owen of the Royal College of Surgeons in London to recognise it in 1839 as coming from a giant bird and later to describe it as *Dinornis novaezealandiae*.

From Tolaga Bay the road again turns inland, following the Hikuwai River as far as The Three Bridges, then descends to Tokomaru Bay. Willows and poplars have been planted along the river courses here in many places, and have colonised others themselves, but they have done little to prevent erosion.

Paradise shelducks are scattered everywhere, living in pairs or in small groups wherever there is water. They gather in large groups after breeding, being particularly partial to areas where maize has been harvested.

The road turns inland again from Tokomaru Bay and travels through hilly country, much of it in sheep and beef cattle farms, not reaching the coast again until Te Araroa.

Mt Hikurangi, the highest point of the Raukumara Range, lies inland from Ruatoria, 40 km north of Tokomaru Bay. Hikurangi was held by the local Ngati-Porou to be the resting place of the canoe of the legendary Maui and said to be inhabited by a giant moa which stood on one leg and fed upon the wind. The mountain was held in such awe that few ventured near and when in the 1830s a Pakeha trader travelled through this area he reported that the countryside around the mountain was pathless and filled with birds and lizards considered by Maori to be spirits.

From Hikurangi came one of the last mainland sightings of the saddleback and in the 1960s members of the Gisborne tramping club heard what they thought may have been the booming of kakapo. Certainly if huia, piopio or kakapo survive in the North Island, it is most likely to be here in the rugged Raukumara Range. This country is very wild and was the last forested area in the North Island to be invaded by feral animals, the Motu River acting as a natural barrier to their spread eastward.

After Ruatoria the road continues its inland course, the countryside alternating between forest and farm with the dividing line not always clear. The falcon is still sometimes to be seen hunting along the forest margins but is nowhere common. Sadly many locals think that the 'sparrowhawk' takes domestic poultry and shoot it on sight.

At Te Araroa, the road reaches the coast again and from here the road turns west to the Bay of Plenty. At Te Araroa itself is found 'Te Waha o Rerekohu', a pohutukawa said by the locals to be the largest in New Zealand, but in fact the one on Mayor Island/Tuhua is larger. The tree takes its name from a large 'pataka', or storehouse, that once stood nearby. As myrtle rust is now appearing in the area, the local iwi is justifiably concerned about the tree's health.

From Te Araroa, a no exit road follows the beach to East Cape lighthouse. The road provides an opportunity to see various seabirds, including gannets, petrels, oystercatchers and several species of terns.

From Hicks Bay, 10 km past Te Araroa, to Whangaparaoa Bay, just south of Cape Runaway, the road takes its last, lengthy inland leg through scrub dominated by gorse. About halfway between the two bays is the Oweka River and for once the name is not a memorial – weka are said to be in the area further up the river. A road follows the Oweka River up to the Waikura Valley where there is good bush with kiwi, kaka, falcons and kakariki, together with a number of the smaller native species. The bush here is rugged so don't go tramping by yourself.

A short side road off SH35 past Potaka leads to Lottin Point where one of the few inland nesting colonies of seabirds survive. Both grey-faced petrels and southern fairy prion have been reported nesting over the years, but their numbers are very low and it would seem only a matter of time before they disappear.

Fur seals haul themselves out on some of the more isolated rocks along this coast, and sea leopards and very occasionally sea elephants have been reported on some of the beaches, up from their sub-Antarctic breeding grounds. Blue penguins (korora), too, are to be seen here and they regularly trudge their way inland to their nesting burrows, which are sometimes as much as a kilometre from the sea and often high above sea level. If you meet these little guys trudging nestward, give them right of way.

Whangaparaoa means the bay of the sperm whale and Maori tradition says it was here that the first canoes, *Arawa* and *Tainui*, landed on arriving from Hawaiki. When they landed, a stranded whale was found on the beach and the captains of the canoes, in order to claim it, argued over who had landed first. Eventually, the captain of the *Arawa* conceded the whale and the land to the *Tainui* and sailed off to settle elsewhere. (The wife of Hoturoa, the captain of the *Tainui*, is credited with introducing kumara to this country.)

At Waihau Bay, where it is possible to hire a dinghy, the hapuka fishing is very good. Once crayfish were so abundant here the local hotel served them for lunch every day, the proprietor catching all he needed in rock pools at low tide.

From here to Opotiki the road skirts the coast and the drive along the rugged coastline is beautiful. In December scarlet pohutukawa and golden lupins line the beaches and the deep blue waters of the many bays provide a marvellous backdrop.

Whanarua Bay is an excellent spot for snorkelling, the many rocky reefs boasting a variety of fish. Terns nest in large numbers among the rocks at the western end of the beach.

One distinction of this area is its rare plants. A member of the plantain family, *Plantago picta* forms attractive mats on the rapidly eroding mudstone cliffs. Another of our rarest plants, known only from near Opape farther along the coast, is *Carmichaelia williamsii*, a particularly attractive member of the broom family.

Shellfish are common all along the East Coast and this area is also a popular destination for anglers. Seaweed is a rather novel product here and substantial quantities are harvested and sent to Opotiki for processing.

Te Kaha, once a dairying area, is today a flourishing horticultural centre. Up to the 1920s whaling was also important. The local Te Whanau-a-Apanui had their own whaling business and used to row out from shore in pursuit of migrating whales (the last was hand-harpooned here in 1925). For many years two ribs from a whale formed an archway in front of a local church, but these have now been moved to the Whakatane Museum.

From Te Kaha it is only a drive of 9 km to Omaio. Here the Haparapara River (which joins the Waikakariki River before flowing into Omaio Bay) is considered to be of particular importance by biologists as it is one of the last remaining river systems without introduced fish. This gives them an opportunity to study freshwater fauna, such as the galaxiid fishes, unaffected by foreign competition.

It is less than 10km from Omaio to the Motu, the principal river of the region. One meaning of Motu is "isolated" and it certainly is, rising in the rugged Raukumaras and winding its tortuous way to the sea through some of the most rugged, trackless bush found anywhere in Aotearoa. The river provides canoeing and rafting trips and once each year a run of kahawai occurs off the river mouth

Although game was late arriving here it is now prolific and causing extensive damage to the bush in the hinterland. Massive slips and erosion have resulted, causing great amounts of sediment to flow into the Motu, killing off much of the aquatic life. Red deer, pigs, goats and feral cattle are now all found here, along with countless numbers of possums and this area is now a popular destination for hunters. The pigs are particularly sought after, but any resemblance between these animals and the domesticated Landrace or Tamworth is remote indeed.

From the Motu the road runs through farmland, but the brooding presence of the Raukumara Ranges is a constant backdrop. At Opape, where the coast ends, at low tide it is possible to walk around the rocks and many shells can be found on the beach. Most are bivalves but good specimens of volutes and several other species are also to be found. A walk around the rocks will also take you to cliffs where nesting black-backed gulls and various shags can be seen on the cliff ledges or in the pohutukawa shaggery overhanging the sea. Of interest to plant enthusiasts, also found here at Opape, is one of our rarest plants, the thick-leaved tree daisy (akiraho), *Olearia pachyphylla,* which has never been found anywhere else. There are labelled specimens planted along the nearby cliff top as well as specimens in the Hukutaia Domain not far outside Opotiki. There are also a number of rare ferns. The royal fern *Todea barbara* and the coastal brake *Pteris carsei* have both been collected here.

After Opape the typical East Coast scenery ends and a drive of about 20 km through farmland will take you to Opotiki, and the beginning of the Bay of Plenty.

CHAPTER 9

Bay of Plenty/Te Moana a Toi and Coromandel

The Bay of Plenty was given its name by Captain Cook in 1769 because of the abundant provisions he obtained from the Maori villages here. This immense crescent of land, backed throughout almost its entire length by the brooding greywacke Kaimai and Raukumara ranges, has long been a generous provider.

The large areas of flat land, once cleared of their forest cover, were long dominated by dairying but in recent years the bay's warm climate and regular rainfall have been fully exploited by the horticultural industry. Large areas of land, particularly around Opotiki in the east and Tauranga and Te Puke in the west, are now devoted to horticulture.

From Matawai, SH2 turns first west and then north again towards Opotiki. Near Wairata, 40 km south-east of Opotiki, the bush returns. At this altitude of almost 800 m the typical rimu-rata-tawa bush of the lower altitudes gives way to the rimu-beech forests of the mountains. The birds here are a mixed lot: kereru, tui, bellbirds, tits, robins and falcons can all be found, together with kaka, whiteheads and riflemen – although these last three species are now diminishing in numbers.

Wairata is also a good area for spotting the blue duck or whio. A lover of fast-flowing waters, the whio has a fairly restricted habitat. If you get a chance, see if you can find one in some of the tributary streams that flow into the Waioweka River. This is not easy because its blue-grey plumage blends in well with the background boulders and it has a habit of riding the rapids rather than flying. Be careful as waters here rise rapidly and if crossing private land be sure to get the landowner's permission.

After Wairata the Waioweka Scenic Highway follows the right bank of the Waioweka River virtually all the way to Opotiki through some fine stands of native forest. The name Waioeka seems to be a corrupted form of Waioweka (water of the weka) and although weka disappeared from here in the 1920s a few have recently returned to the upper reaches of the river, from Poverty Bay, and are now spreading out into the Bay of Plenty.

Ancient pa sites have recently been found in this inland area. From midden remains, archaeologists have determined that they were apparently built by Maori engaged in collecting shearwater (muttonbird) chicks during their annual nesting season. Now, most people associate shearwaters with coastal areas, but presumably several species once flew far inland to nest, navigating among these rugged peaks at night.

The Tuhoe of the Urewera Ranges made mention of the calls they made at night flying overhead. In the Inland Kaikouras and on the West Coast of the South Island some still fly inland.

Today extensive possum damage is obvious in this forest and foresters estimate that about a third of the kamahi in the Waioweka and neighbouring areas have died, together with many rata. Although possum trappers help to keep animal numbers down, their complete eradication now seems impossible. A sign of high possum numbers in any area is stainless steel bands on the electricity poles. These are put there to prevent possums climbing the poles and disrupting the local power supply while frying themselves in the process.

Lamprey, koaro, banded kokopu, both species of eel and inanga are among the native fish of the Waioweka, together with the introduced brown and rainbow trout. One of the last examples of the now extinct native grayling (upokororo) was taken from the Waioweka in 1904. This fish was considered so unusual it was paraded around the hotels in Opotiki.

After leaving the Waioweka Gorge, a straight stretch of road of almost 10 km heads towards Opotiki. Not surprisingly, this is called the Waioweka Straight and along it stands a number of fine exotic trees, many planted last century, several by my forebears.

It was near Opotiki that I spent much of my early life, and it was here that I first heard stories of the former birdlife that once flourished in our bush. Ronny Campbell, a forester who was brought up at Pakihi, recalls meeting a group of 11 kokako moving single file through the Pakihi bush in the late 1950s and believes he heard a laughing owl (whekau) in the same area some 10 years earlier. Having worked many years in the bush, he has a good knowledge of most of the forested country of the East Cape.

Some of the largest known specimens of kahikatea are found behind Pakihi at Te Waiti and there are also extensive stands here of matai, tawa and rimu. Rather confusingly, bellbirds are called mockingbirds in this area; this is probably a corruption of their Maori name makomako; because mockingbirds they most certainly are not!

Seven kilometers west of Opotiki along the Woodlands Road is Hukutaia Domain. This magnificent 4.5 ha of bush is centred around 'Taketakerau', a puriri tree sacred to the local Whakatohea people and one of New Zealand's oldest trees, estimated to be about 2,000 years old. Here, until the arrival of Pakeha, the bones of distinguished dead were placed with appropriate ceremonies inside the tree's hollow trunk. It is believed as many as 200 skeletons were once interred here.

From 1940, over a period of about 30 years, a keen amateur botanist, Norman Potts, a local lawyer, planted in the Hukutaia Domain a large number of trees and shrubs he had collected, along with other plants sent to him by fellow enthusiasts from around the country. Today there are trees, shrubs and grasses at Hukutaia from all parts of New Zealand with specimens from as far afield as the Chathams and the Kermedecs growing side by side. It is considered New Zealand's best collection of endemic trees. However, the Domain nowadays is concentrating on local material. If you visit Hukutaia make sure to check out the magnificent king ferns (para) growing just inside the gates. They were collected by Potts in the nearby Waioweka Gorge but have now long gone from there. Also visit the historic puriri Taketakerau in the centre of the domain.

At Kukumoa, about four kilometers west of Opotiki on SH2, once stood the large, fortified Ngati Awa pa called Tawhitinui. The pa is of interest for the battle that was fought over a tame tui once kept here. This bird belonged to a chief called Kahukino and was an especially gifted mimic which could recite many charms and spells. This excited the admiration of a Ngati-Ha visitor from Waiaua, who asked to be given the bird. Kahukino refused, so some time later the visitor returned to attack the pa and capture it. The defeated Tawhitinui people were forced to flee to the Gisborne area.

Tui are well known for their ability as mimics and one of the earliest commentators to remark on this was Dr Ernst Dieffenbach who noted:

> *He has a soft fluting voice, which re-echoes in the forest from morning to the evening. His imitative faculty is remarkable. I heard one that barked like a dog, another that crowed like a cock, and a third that talked long phrases.*

Some of these phrases were long indeed. Elsdon Best, who spent many years among Tuhoe of the Urewera, detailed a number of the chants, or karakia, that tui were said to recite. He also wrote that only the male tui made a good talker and that attempting to teach the female to speak was a waste of time.

On the coast north-east of Opotiki cattle egret (kotuku) once wintered over each year, among a herd of grazing dairy cattle, between April and October. However they departed suddenly and permanently several decades ago. They may have been spooked by large scale earthworks in the bed of the nearby Waioweka River but the exact cause was never determined.

Bitterns have also been seen here in the ditches where they hunt eels and tadpoles, quite a change from their usual haunts, and their booming calls can sometimes be heard at night.

From Kukumoa SH2 travels along the Waiotahe (formerly Waiotahi) Beach before turning inland again just after crossing the Waiotahe River. This beach road passes through some particularly fine examples of pohutukawa, and on clear days White Island/Whakaari can be seen in the distance with its plume of white steam. White Island, despite its threatening appearance, and occasional deadly eruptions, is home to large numbers of nesting petrels as well as one of our largest colonies of gannets. These seabirds must be rugged individuals as land birds which stray to the island often succumb to the toxic fumes.

After crossing the Waiotahe Bridge a sharp turn right will take you to the Ohiwa Harbour. The harbour, beautifully situated amid rolling bush and farm-covered hills, is of recent geological origin and only 5,000 years ago it was a bay facing the ocean.

Because of the mild climate, mangroves (paetai) are found here and the trees near the entrance of the harbour are the most southerly mangroves in the world.

Each year thousands of eastern bar-tailed godwits fly here from their nesting grounds in Alaska 12,000 km away, arriving in a large flock at Ohiwa around October and heading off again in April or May. At low tide they scatter around the harbour to feed, but at high tide they congregate together on the islands in the middle of the harbour where they can rest undisturbed. Other waders can also be seen here; indeed, the second recorded sighting in New Zealand of an American whimbrel was made at Ohiwa Harbour in 1949 when a bird spent the summer in the company of godwits. Red knots (huahou) and ruddy turnstones are probably the most numerous migrants here after the godwits.

Of interest on Whangakopikopiko/Tern Island in the middle of the harbour there is a mixed flock of red-billed (tarapunga) and black-billed (tarapuka) gulls along with a few white-fronted terns (tara). In most other parts of the country breeding flocks are segregated. Landing on the island is banned but you can get a good view of the colony from a kayak or boat or if you have a good pair of binoculars from the nearby Ohiwa Spit.

From the harbour the more scenic route is along SH2 which loops through Waimana to Whakatane. A detour 10 km south of Kutarere of some 20 km before you reach Waimana will take you to Tanatana and the northern reaches of Te Urewera. The road follows the Waimana River flowing from the Huiarau Range and good stands of trees, particularly kahikatea, can be seen along the river flats. Huiarau means "many huia", a sad reminder of this now extinct bird.

Another extinct bird that seems to have been present here until fairly recently was the piopio, once called the native thrush. Arthur Taylor, a park ranger who was familiar with the birds of the park, recalled that while he was working on the Six Foot Track near Te Panaa in 1968 a 'stocky dark-brown' bird came to within a couple of metres of him. He was sure that this was a piopio and his description fits both its appearance and its confiding nature.

After the farmland near Waimana township the road moves through scrub and both native and exotic forest. Introduced birds seem to like this area and in autumn and winter large flocks of finches, including goldfinches, redpolls, yellowhammers, chaffinches and greenfinches can be seen.

Greenfinches are often called linnets, which they are not. The linnet was introduced here, but being a migratory bird probably disappeared towards Japan when the first winter came.

My grandfather Philip Farnworth, who lived in Whakatane and was involved in bird rescue notably of kiwi and penguins, told me that in the part of England he came from the yellowhammer was called the master scribbler. A glance at the enchanting pattern on their eggs shows where this name originated. A poem by John Clare describes this:

> *Five eggs, pen scribbled o'er with ink their shells,*
> *Resembling writing scrolls, which Fancy reads*
> *As Nature's poesy and pastoral spells –*
> *They are the yellowhammer's and she dwells*
> *Most poet like, 'mid brooks and flowery weeds.*

From Whakatane it was once possible to charter a helicopter to White/Whakaari Island, but this was discontinued after the deadly 2019 eruption and it may be some time before it recommences. Also, from Whakatane's foreshore good views can be had of Whale Island/Moutohora to the north-east.

Among the 'muttonbirds' that nest on Whale Island are the sooty shearwater (hakoakoa), the fluttering shearwater (pakaha), the grey-faced petrel (oi) and Buller's shearwater (rako). These were all traditionally harvested by the Ngati Awa of Whakatane but falling numbers caused a rahui, or tribal protection, to be placed on the remaining birds. Also look out for grey noddies which breed on islets in the Bay of Plenty.

For many years this island supported large numbers of goats, thousands of rabbits and multitudes of rats, all of which did incalculable damage both to the fauna and the vegetation. After the government purchased the island from its private owners the goats were culled and the rabbits poisoned. An unexpected and most welcome side effect of the poisoning was that the rats disappeared – presumably after dining on the rabbits. Consequently, Whale Island is the largest island in mainland New Zealand to be totally cleared of vermin and its prospects look hopeful. Replanting trees to replace those killed off by goats is underway and kakariki and tieke have been released on the island. The island is a kiwi creche but being nocturnal you are unlikely to see these. There is also a fur seal (kekeno) colony on this island.

From Whakatane, SH2 follows the coast road through the farmlands around Thornton to Matata, named for the fernbird which still can be found around the lagoon opposite the town. It is hard now to imagine the mighty Rangitaiki Swamp, which began to be drained for farmland about 1890, for all that remains now are some large ditches.

Black swan are permanent residents of the Matata Lagoon along with many grey ducks, mallards, shovelers and pukeko and occasionally scaup. Large numbers of refugees turn up each shooting season, much to the disgust of frustrated hunters drowning their sorrows at the pub opposite.

About 100 m east of the Awatataraki Stream, between the railway and the main highway, is a large pohutukawa which has a traditional importance for local Maori. It was a resting place for travellers and warriors returning home with bones from battlefields further afield. These grisly remains would be hung from the tree while the war party rested.

From Matata a long straight road takes you west towards Tauranga. This is a pleasant drive with pohutukawa clinging to the cliffs and rows of toetoe and flax between the road and the beach. The kingfisher (kotare) favours the cliff for nesting sites and they sit on the power lines looking for lunch along the roadside verges. Swallows, too, like the cliffs and ceaselessly swoop up and down them chasing insects.

From Matata the road skirts the coast, passing through open farmland until the Kaimai Ranges are reached west of Tauranga. This area has been continuously settled by Pakeha for over 150 years – much of it originally confiscated from local tribes after the New Zealand Wars – and not surprisingly most birds here are exotics: finches, blackbirds, thrushes and starlings along with magpies and mynas.

The long period of European settlement is most clearly evident in Tauranga itself with its fine exotic trees. The macrocarpa on Moffats Road, Bethlehem, is the world's largest and is far taller than any growing on the Monterey Peninsula in California, this tree's natural habitat.

'The Elms', in Tauranga itself, marks the site of the first Anglican mission in the Bay of Plenty and some of the trees date from as early as 1838 and are of considerable size. Nevertheless, the best group of trees is almost certainly that at Yatton Park and these date from plantings between 1865 and 1877 by John Alfred Chadwick, an early farmer. Among the finest of these are a Japanese cedar, a Bhutan cypress, a Canary Island pine, a South Queensland kauri and a Bunya pine.

From Tauranga a trip out to the McLaren Falls Park on the Tauranga Matamata road is rewarding. (Turn off SH29 onto McLaren Falls Road 11 km from Tauranga.) Members of the Bay of Plenty Tree Society have planted about 12,000 trees and these should in time be a splendid collection.

On Mayor Island/Tuhua, offshore from Tauranga, stands what is almost surely the country's largest pohutukawa. This tree stands on a track between South East Bay and North West Bay and when measured in 1982 had a trunk diameter of 3.27 m. The island is a sanctuary for wildlife with large populations of tui, kaka, kereru and korimako.

For a number of years this part of the Bay was patrolled by a pod of 16 orca led by a large male with a distinctive dog-eared dorsal fin. The whales ranged from here to Cape Karikari in the north and to the Mahia Peninsula in the south.

Around Tauranga Harbour itself large numbers of waders congregate, which is surprising considering the number of boats on the harbour. Godwits, oystercatchers, gulls, stilts, terns and occasionally rare waders such as the grey-tailed tattler are to be seen. Groups of shags stand around the stream mouths, looking, in their black and white livery, a little like unemployed waiters. Mt Maunganui, which dominates the harbour, provides a breeding place for grey-faced petrel.

In the Tauranga Harbour it is worthwhile checking to see which waders are present, particularly around the western end of the harbour where kotuku and royal spoonbills are known to feed.

At various points along the highway, roads run up into the hills of the Kaimai-Mamaku Forest Park. There are over 19,000 ha of virgin forest here and the region is the southern limit of the kauri and the northern limit of red and silver beech. Kiwi, kakariki and some smaller birds are to be found together with lizards and bats. Native frogs and kokako occur in the west of the park.

The highest point of the park is Mt Te Aroha on the western side of the range. This is an enchanting place to visit on cloudy days when mist wreaths the 'goblin forest' of kaikawaka, toi, neinei and silver beech. On fine days you can see a great sweep of country from the Hauraki Plains in the north and west to the Bay of Plenty in the east, and as far as Cape Runaway in the south.

To reach the Coromandel Peninsula, take the Whitianga Bay turn-off from Waihi along SH25. From there it is a pleasant drive up the coast through scenery as diverse as anything to be found in the country. High forest-covered ranges, boulder-strewn beaches, pohutukawa-fringed bays, patches of neatly tended farms and estuaries teaming with wading birds are all located within a few kilometres of each other.

Because the Coromandel Peninsula is a sea-gird mountain range it shares many of the characteristics of an island. The vegetation has more in common with that of the neighbouring islands than it does with other mainland regions. Many plants have the northern limit of their range here, while others reach their southern boundaries. This creates a tremendous variation in the Coromandel vegetation which is in keeping with the physical diversity of the peninsula. In stark contrast to the rich subtropical forest of the lower reaches, the mist-shrouded peak of Moehau has plants and trees that would seem more at home on the South Island's West Coast – silver and pink pine, kaikawaka, mountain toatoa, sweet hutu and southern rata.

The Coromandel Range was covered in kauri when Pakeha arrived, but logging started early. The Royal Navy was the first to exploit this resource as the timber was in demand for use as spars in their sailing ships. Wide-scale logging soon followed and this continued until few sizeable trees remained. One that still stands tall is 'Tane Nui' but due to Kauri dieback, access is restricted to this mighty tree.

The largest tree ever recorded in New Zealand was a giant kauri known as "Father of the Forest" which stood near the head of Mill Creek, Mercury Bay. Its girth was recorded as 23.77 m and the height to the first branch was 24.38 m, which would have made it half as big again as the present record holder, 'Tane Mahuta', in the Waipoua Kauri Forest.

On remote ridges there are still to be seen the gaunt skeletons of burnt kauri, too inaccessible for the loggers to retrieve and, here and there, other grand old trees grievously damaged by fire, but still standing to testify to a once-glorious forest. Yet the regenerating forest is rich and diverse: good stands of young kauri seedlings known as rickers flourish along with rimu, totara, tanekaha, rewarewa, rata and a great mass of shrubs and herbs. Be careful when walking through the bush, particularly in areas where there was once gold mining activity. In some places overgrown mine shafts and workings are a trap for the unwary.

The Coromandel is home to a number of endangered species. Small numbers of kaka and kiwi are still found, and native frogs, first found by Pakeha in this area in 1852, survive in a few small colonies. Other bush birds are easier to find. Korimako, tui and kereru occur in most places together with the commoner forest dwellers.

Among the exotics, California quail and pheasants are in good numbers.

The drive along the eastern side of the peninsula takes you through a variety of habitats which permit a diverse range of birds to be seen. This coast is a favoured area for shags, as well as for reef and white-faced herons.

At Whangamata, many waders use the estuary and dotterels, gulls and terns are nearly always present. The Tairua Forest, which edges the town, is all

pine, so few native birds are to be found here except where it adjoins native bush — here you can sometimes find pied tits.

North of the Tairua Forest is the Wharekawa Harbour, another spot popular with waders and waterfowl. The best place to see them is at Opoutere on the harbour's northern side. Here there are shags along with white-faced herons, black swans, mallards, grey ducks and sometimes shovelers. Rarer visitors are kotuku and cattle egrets while banded rail and fernbirds can also be found in suitable cover.

The sand spit at the harbour mouth is a reserve for feeding pairs of dotterels and oystercatchers.

Further up the coast is Mercury Bay where Cook landed and his party observed the transit of the planet Mercury. Joseph Banks was particularly taken with a pa built atop a natural rock arch here at Mercury Bay and it moved him to describe it as '... the most beautifully romantick [sic] thing I ever saw'. Unfortunately it has since disappeared.

From Whitianga it is sometimes possible to take a boat to the Mercury Islands. Many seabirds can be seen from the boat, including gannets and skuas. Petrels and shearwaters are also numerous, but only experts can identify the different species. The Aldermen Islands to the south are home to many tuatara.

If you wish to travel on to the Moehau Range you will need to cross to the western side of the peninsula. Mt Moehau, at 892 m, is the tallest peak in the Range. If you can cope with a strenuous day's climb you will be rewarded with the most spectacular views of the Coromandel. The Moehau Range is also noteworthy for the rare native frog *Leiopelma archeyi*, sometimes seen here, whose young hatch from eggs, bypassing the tadpole stage. It also has a rare stag beetle, *Geodorcus sp.* 'Moehau'.

The harbour at Port Charles is connected by walking tracks to the coast road around the west of Moehau. It is a four hour tramp with wonderful sea views and many seabirds to be seen.

Because of Coromandel's equable climate, kingfishers (kotare) flock here in winter for the insects and crustacea they need to sustain themselves during the cold weather. These birds are particularly plentiful in the pohutukawa along the coastal beaches. Kotare were considered by the Maori to be unlucky and if a war party came across one the ensuing battle would be called off. As several dozen kotare can be seen in an hour's walk along Coromandel's beaches, this area might well have suited a tribe of a peaceful disposition.

Offshore from the town of Coromandel itself, as well as off Manaia, there are many islands and rock stacks, several of which have breeding colonies of gannets or ganneteries. Also breeding are blue penguins, grey-faced storm petrels, white-faced storm petrels, diving petrels, gulls, terns and shags.

The area south of Coromandel was once the scene of intense gold mining activity which, together with logging, has left a tremendous amount of environmental damage. Now multinational companies are talking about resuming mining here, spouting all the usual platitudes about protecting the environment. But if in the wide open spaces of countries such as Australia and South Africa the effects of strip mining are bad, here on the Coromandel, with its physical diversity and fragile, and often unstable, terrain they would be disastrous.

From Coromandel township south to Thames the road is sealed and is an easy drive. It follows the coastline, so unless you make a detour along a side road you will see mostly wading and seabirds.

After passing through Thames the road crosses the Waihou River not far from where it flows into the Firth of Thames. Cook travelled up the Waihou River as far as he could get in a longboat looking for timber suitable for ship building. He found large stands of kahikatea, which Banks described:

> 'The banks of the river were completely cloathed with the finest timber my eyes ever beheld of a tree we had seen before, but only at a distance in Poverty Bay, Hawke's Bay....thick woods of it everywhere, every tree as straight as pencil and of immense size.'

These trees were all logged out in the late 1890s. After crossing the Waihou the road traverses the Hauraki Plains toward Auckland.

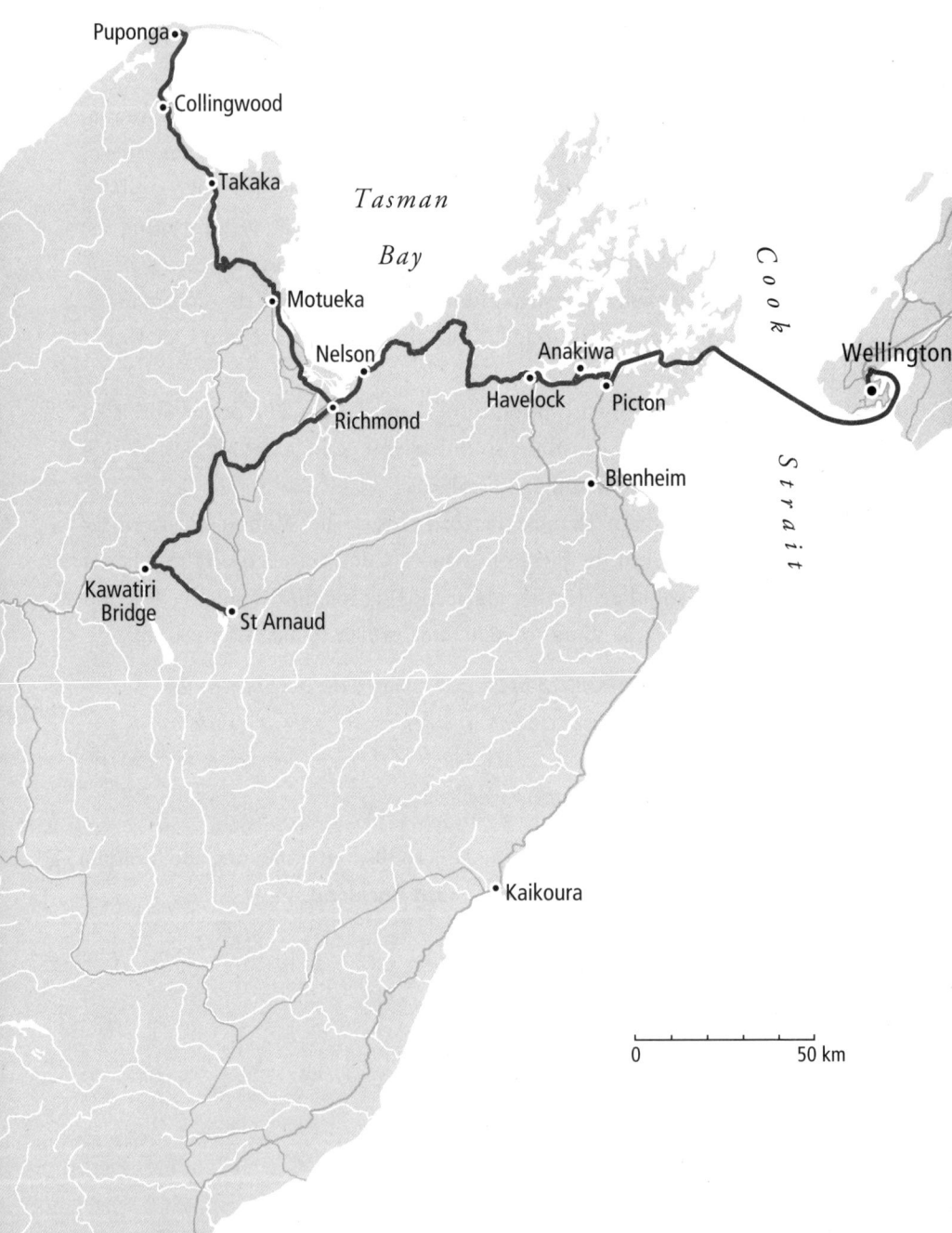

CHAPTER 10

Nelson and Marlborough/Te Tau Ihu

The labyrinth of islands and peninsulas that make up the Marlborough Sounds is the first sight travellers have of the South Island when arriving by ferry from Wellington. The sounds are the northernmost extension of the Richmond Range, an alternating series of many-branched narrow valleys and sharp-topped ridges drowned since the end of the last Ice Age. The shelter offered by this maze of sounds and islands attracted early European navigators and much of the South Island's first scientific research was done here.

Cook was probably the first European to sail into the Sounds. Arriving on 15 January 1770, he needed to careen and clear his boat of marine growths and found the ideal place at what is now called Ship Cove, off Queen Charlotte Sound. It is known as Totaranui in Maori for its large stands of this fine canoe-building timber.

It was here on the first morning at anchor that the ship's company was 'awakened by the singing of birds ashore'. Such magnificent dawn choruses are no longer and, ironically, it was probably rats which went ashore from the Endeavour while it was being careened that started the demise of the birdlife here.

While here, Joseph Banks and Daniel Solander spent their time ashore collecting specimens of both plants and animals, although both noted that the vegetation was a little disappointing. Among the birds collected were 'three birds having wattles,' and it has been suggested that these were a saddleback, kokako and huia. However, as the huia was confined to the North Island, the third bird was probably an immature saddleback (in the South Island the juvenile, sometimes called the Jack Bird, differs so much from the adult that some early Pakeha regarded it as a distinct species).

On 18 May 1773, during his second voyage to the Pacific, Cook returned to Ship Cove. With him on this voyage he had a new ship scientist, the German Johann Reinhold Forster, who was accompanied by his son Johann Georg Adam Forster as his artist. The Forster party collected the morepork, the falcon and two species of shag. They also took the first recorded native land mammal – the long-tailed bat (pekapeka-tou-roa).

It was in Queen Charlotte Sound that, with the best possible intentions and among the worst possible results, Cook made the first deliberate release of land mammals in this country (geese were liberated earlier at Goose Cove, in Fiordland). Near Ship Cove, Cook set free pigs, sheep and goats. The sheep quickly died, causing Cook to report sadly:

> Last night the Ewe and Ram I had with much trouble brought to this place, died, we did suppose they were poisoned by eating some poisonous plant, thus all my fine hopes of stocking this Country with a breed of sheep were blasted in a moment.

The liberation of pigs and goats also had its setbacks. He released a boar and two sows, and a few days later a pair of goats, with the comment:

> There is no great danger that the Natives will destroy them as they are exceedingly afraid of both... The goats will undoubtedly take to the Mountains and the Hoggs [sic] to the Woods where there is plenty of food.

Any fear the local Maori had of these animals was quickly allayed – when Cook returned six months later all but one sow had been eaten. Only slightly deterred Cook released more animals and from these most of the wild goats and pigs noted by the early Pakeha settlers in the South Island were descended.

In late May 1820, the Imperial Russian ships the *Vostok* and the *Mirnyi*, under Captain Fabian Gottlieb von Bellingshausen, arrived. The Russians did some collecting here, taking tui, pigeons, parakeets and falcons as well as a number of ducks, seabirds and shags.

The next scientific party to come to this area was French, in 1826 on *L'Astrolabe*, under the command of Dumont D'Urville who was on his second voyage to New Zealand, having visited the Bay of Islands some years earlier.

The French concentrated on the large island to the west now named for D'Urville and known in Maori as Rangitoto ki te Tonga.

Unlike Banks and von Bellingshausen, D'Urville found the bush strangely quiet:

> *No birds, no insects, no reptiles even, this complete absence of any living creature and the unbroken silence create a solemn, almost sinister atmosphere. Going through these gloomy, solitary places, one felt as if one were transported to the point in time when nature, having produced the members of the vegetable kingdom, still waited for the decree of the Eternal, to bring forth the living creatures.*

Despite these observations the expedition scientists, Jean-Renee Quoy and Joseph Paul Gaimard, collected numerous birds here, including kaka, kokako, tui and two previously unknown species, the South Island fernbird (matata) and the grey warbler (riroriro).

D'Urville Island was once mooted as an island sanctuary, similar to Kapiti and Little Barrier islands. It was here one of two populations of little spotted kiwi (kiwi pukupuku) had survived after vanishing from the mainland. In the 1970s it was found that because of predation by cats and stoats only three birds remained on D'Urville and these were taken off the island. A pair was sent to Maud Island/Te Hoiere, but by 1982 stoats had followed them even there, so the surviving female was moved yet again to Long Island/Kokomohua. Takahe were also released on Maud but were later removed because of predators.

Due north of D'Urville Island is Stephens Island/Takapourewa, notable among other things for the dubious fame achieved by the lighthouse keeper's cat, Tibbles. In 1894 this animal brought in 11 specimens of an unknown wren (kotipatipa), which was quickly recognised as a new species. Not quickly enough however, as within a very short time Tibbles had destroyed the entire population. Recent fossil finds indicate that this bird had relatives on the mainland before Pakeha arrived which were probably wiped out by the Polynesian rat (kiore).

Stephens Island is also home to the country's largest population of tuatara. This animal is not a lizard, as most people think, but the sole survivor of an ancient reptile order called the *Rhynchocephalia*, or beakheads, which died out elsewhere 60 million years ago. About 50,000 tuatara – at least half the known population – are found here, and these were looked after by the lighthouse keepers (who no longer have cats). With the automation of lighthouses it was feared that the tuatara population would be vulnerable to poaching by reptile collectors, so DoC stationed a ranger on the island.

Stephens Island also boasts the native Stephens Island frog *Leiopelma hamiltoni*, (pepeke), a giant weta *Deinacrida rugosa* and a healthy population of lizards – one unique, the Stephens Island gecko, *Toropuka stephensi*. A number of seabirds that are scarce elsewhere nest on Stephens Island. The island is riddled with the burrows of fairy prion (titi wainui) which they share with the tuatara.

At the entrance to Queen Charlotte Sound are colonies of about 500 of our rarest shag, the king shag (kawau pateketeke). Being related to shags which frequent sub-Antarctic waters, the king shag beats its wings to dry them unlike most other shags. Presumably they would have been waiting a long time in the sub-Antarctic for the sun to dry them out.

The next sound west of Queen Charlotte is Pelorus – the former haunt of Pelorus Jack. Pelorus Jack was a Risso's dolphin which, between 1888 and 1912, accompanied any steamer travelling outside Admiralty Bay and Pelorus Sound. In 1904 a law was passed to protect him after someone tried to shoot him from a passing steamer. He was last seen in April 1912 and various rumours surrounded his disappearance.

However, subsequent research has shown that Pelorus Jack was an old animal. His head was white and his body pale, both indications of age, so it can be assumed he died of natural causes. The Risso's dolphin is a rare species in New Zealand waters, and it is possible he swam alongside ships for company in the absence of his own kind.

Other more common dolphin species are often found in these waters. Bottle-nosed, common and dusky dolphins are all regulars, and this is the northernmost range of the beautiful Hector's (or New Zealand) dolphin.

The Marlborough Sounds have also hosted whalers – the station at Te Awaiti in Tory Channel was built in the mid 1820s to harvest right whales and humpbacks migrating through Cook Strait. In 1911 the Perano family who ran the station introduced fast motor launches equipped with explosive-headed harpoons, which greatly increased their catch. The addition of a mothership chaser meant more than 200 humpbacks a year could be taken and enabled sperm and occasionally blue whales to be hunted further offshore. These local operations, and the relentless operations of foreign whalers, nearly exterminated New Zealand's whale stocks. In the early 1950s more than 500 humpback whale were counted on their annual migration through Cook Strait, but by 1963 only 23 were seen.

Large numbers of different seabirds can be seen from the inter-island ferry depending on the distance from port. Giant petrels or stinkpots (pangurunguru) were abundant once around the old whaling station where up to 200 at a time fed on offal and previously some followed the inter-island ferries feeding on waste from the ships. Penguins are also a common sight and I have even spotted them under the wharf at Picton. Visits to the islands of the Marlborough Sounds can be arranged with boat operators in Picton. Islands worth visiting include Motuara and Oruawairua also known as Blumine Island. Motuara has good numbers of birds. Tieke and South Island robin (toutouwai) have both been reintroduced to Motuara and the robins are very friendly. One perched on my boot when I was taking a breather. Motuara is also a creche for the rowi and these kiwi spend a few months here bulking up before being returned to their home territory at Okarito. You are unlikely to see rowi although it is sometimes possible to glimpse their bottoms in crevices or burrows while they are snoozing. Definitely no 'selfies'. There are also native frogs (pepeketua). From the boat king shags can sometimes be seen but visits to the breeding colonies are banned.

Oruawairua/Blumine is another island well worth visiting. Here there is a reasonably good chance of seeing our rarest forest bird, the orange-fronted kakariki (kakariki karaka) along with tieke, weka, South Island tomtits (ngirungiru) and maybe mohua. Rowi are here also but you would need to camp overnight and the chance of seeing these is not great. However, they are showing signs of breeding.

If you are short of time, then you should spend a bit of time at the Pelorus Bridge Reserve which is 19 km from Havelock along SH6 to Nelson. It is well signposted and has a good population of birds.

There are also many walkways through the Sounds and these can be explored using Picton as a base.

Three longer walks are the Nydia Track, the Anakiwa Track and the Endeavour to Ship Cove Track. The Nydia Track is reached by crossing the Pelorus River about 2.5 km past Canvastown on SH6. Across the bridge turn hard right and take the rough road to Kaiuma Bay about 15 km distance. The track itself runs from Kaiuma Farm to Tennyson Inlet and takes about eight to nine hours. From high points on the track good views can be had south to the Kaikoura Ranges and Mt Tapuaenuku and north to Nydia Bay.

There was once thick forest all through this area but logging has removed all the larger trees from the accessible areas between Kaiuma Farm and Nydia Bay. From Nydia Bay to Tennyson Inlet the track, after running through considerable areas of scrub and regenerating forest, passes through some good stands of large rimu, kahikatea, pukatea and mahoe, along with flourishing growths of nikau. There is also a fine variety of ferns.

The track from Anakiwa to Portage is part of the Queen Charlotte Track, is about 19 km long and takes 6 to 7 hours to walk. (You will need a Pass from DoC to complete this walk.) It starts from Anakiwa Bay, past the Outward Bound School, which is reached by turning off the Picton to Havelock road just past Okiwa Bay, some 18 km from Picton. An early visitor, Colonel William Wakefield, noted the magnificent forest here but almost 100 years of milling put paid to that.

At one time, almost 10,000 feet of timber was being milled daily by four mills in this area. The track to Davies Bay takes you through small patches of forest, but more extensive areas are found along the track above Bottle Bay, Puroa and Hou Hou points, which also give splendid views of Queen Charlotte

Sound. Around Te Mahia the bush starts to thin out again, giving way to scrub and pasture, with only occasional stands of trees, mostly around the gullies.

The Endeavour Inlet to Ship Cove Track is also part of the Queen Charlotte Track and best reached by boat from Picton. This track passes through attractive stands of bush on its descent to the coast and from Camp Bay it follows the coast through stands of manuka and tree fern to Big Bay, which still has much of its original bush cover.

From here to the head of Endeavour Inlet you pass through regenerating bush with some smallholdings. In the hills behind the bay there was once a thriving community working the antimony deposits in the surrounding area. Moving on from the inlet takes you through coastal bush and after crossing over a small river you arrive at Howden Bush, a fine stand of mixed podocarp-beech forest. From here you turn inland to Tawa Bay and Ship Cove.

From Picton, several launch trips are available to the Sounds and travelling among the maze of hills and islands rising steeply from the blue green waters is fascinating. There are numerous settlements and small farms around Picton, many accessible only by boat.

Perhaps no other area in the whole country has been so mistreated by bad farming. Continual firing of scrub, little or no fencing or fertiliser and the browsing of trees and shrubs by goats and other stock all contributed to its scrubby appearance. There are also extensive patches of exotic and native bush, but much of the latter is light and supports few native birds.

From Picton the most direct route to Nelson is the coastal road via Linkwater to Havelock. This is 35 km and about 40 minutes' drive, the road giving good views down both Queen Charlotte and Mahau Sounds. At Havelock you rejoin SH6 and from here the 75 km to Nelson is an easy drive of about an hour. The road goes through Rai Valley, past the farming country of the Whangamoa Valley, then over the Whangamoa Saddle into Nelson, the horticultural centre of the South Island.

Nelson was the port of arrival for many of the first European settlers in the South Island. Many came via Australia and the trees they brought were often gums.

The first of these was a Tasmanian blue gum dating from about 1843, which is still thriving. You can see it a short distance above the high water mark at the Wairau Bar, near the mouth of the Wairau River, close to Blenheim.

The first domestic animals were imported by George Duppa, who arrived in Nelson in June 1842 from New South Wales, bringing with him 189 sheep and some Durham cattle settling with these near the Waimea River. A considerably larger shipment was made by Charles Bidwell, who came in 1843 in the schooner *Posthumous*, bringing with him 1,600 sheep and some horses which were landed on Haulashore Island in Nelson Harbour.

No sooner had these immigrants settled than they began 'improving' the wildlife with a gusto encountered in few other parts of the country. Red deer first arrived in Nelson in 1853, when the survivor of a pair sent by the Prince Consort arrived on the *Eagle*. Three replacements were sent on the *Donna Anita*, arriving in 1860. These were released in the hills behind the town and bred rapidly. The first fallow deer to be imported also came to Nelson in 1864 and were released in the Aniseed Valley.

However, it was with exotic birds that the Nelsonites really excelled themselves. In 1862 the first shipment of birds, all caught around London, were liberated in Nelson. They included 26 blackbirds, 5 thrushes and 16 starlings, along with rooks and various finches. Skylarks followed in 1864 and very soon became a pest to local farmers by pulling up sprouting wheat. Californian quail followed the next year.

There is now little native fauna and forest to be seen around the settled areas of Nelson. To best experience what is left, take the road north-west to Abel Tasman National Park, or go further on either to the Kahurangi National Park or Farewell Spit.

From Riwaka to Collingwood the road is sealed, but the climb up over the Takaka Hills is fairly tortuous, so it is definitely not a good idea to stop and sightsee. The descent to Golden Bay is particularly interesting if you are towing a caravan. Allow between 75 and 90 minutes for the trip. At the top of the hill rather bizarre gravestone-like outcrops of marble have lent the name Marble Hill to the area. The descent down the hill takes you first through stands of the large-leafed shrub *Senecio hectori* and then through beech forest.

Time permitting, take a detour up the road from Upper Takaka to the Cobb Reservoir. This road is a bit tricky, so take it carefully. It ends about 1,100 m up and there is a good chance here for you to examine mountain vegetation. If you have come from the North Island this will probably be the first time you will meet that feisty character of the mountains, the kea. Also around here are western weka and a host of smaller birds.

Back on the main road your next stop should be the Abel Tasman National Park which you can reach through Takaka and Motupipi. Turn right at the entrance to Takaka and you're heading directly for Golden Bay. Go through Pohara and past the remnants of the Golden Bay cement works, past Wainui Inlet and over the Pigeon Saddle, then down to Totaranui and its beautiful golden sands.

Established in 1942 on the tri-centenary of Abel Tasman's discovery of New Zealand, the park is among the South Island's most beautiful. Parts of the original forest were burned, to be replaced by dense stands of manuka, gorse, bracken and pine, but the forest is slowly reasserting itself. Much of it is steep, broken country where the soft, golden granite has been worked by water into a myriad of shapes. Rivers slice through it before dropping into an azure sea fringed with golden beaches. It is the interplay of ocean and land which contributes so much to the beauty of the Abel Tasman Park, so it is ironic that it ends abruptly at the water's edge. It is essentially a coastal park and it would be logical to extend protection to the adjoining waters. Because of its beauty and ease of access it is one of the most popular holiday destinations in the South Island and has become a centre for tramping, boating and swimming.

From the Park the road continues north-west around Golden Bay/Mohua. Tasman originally named it Murderers' Bay for an unhappy encounter with the local Ngati Tumatakokiri but in the late 1850s the name was changed to Golden Bay when gold was discovered at Aorere. Settlement here is mainly along the coast and up the valleys along the Aorere and Takaka rivers.

The area has been connected with the North Island several times in the recent geological past and this dry land bridge allowed the two-way migration of plants and animals. The bay also served as a *refugia* for southern species during the ice ages and so this region today is home to a wide variety of flora and fauna.

Behind Golden Bay lies the North-West Nelson Forest Park and from Collingwood a drive of 30 km takes you to the start of the Heaphy Track, near the confluence of the Brown and Aorere rivers.

Despite the damage caused by browsing animals the vegetation of the park is still in good condition. This forest has the usual altitudinal variation, with podocarp in the lowlands gradually changing to beech, before giving way to alpine herb fields on the tops of the ranges. Two botanical highlights of the park are the extensive stands of nikau on the alluvial flats in the Kohaihai-Heaphy area and the pukatea in the gullies in the north.

Increasing numbers of trampers are now coming to this region, drawn by the large number of walking tracks many of which follow tracks first opened up by goldminers and explorers. The best known is the track named for the artist and explorer Charles Heaphy, which runs from Brown Hut (30 kms from Collingwood) to Kohaihai, north of Karamea on the West Coast.

This is a comfortable four to six day walk with huts no more than seven walking hours apart. From the end of the road the track goes steadily upwards through beech forest before moving out onto the open, rolling Gouland Downs, an extensive plain of red tussock. And because the trail was originally cut for packhorses it is fairly easy going. In the half-light of dawn and dusk, with clouds banking up and rolling across the moody skies, this area has an eerie, almost sinister quality about it.

At first glance the country seems to have a uniform cover of uninterrupted red tussock but closer examination reveals an astonishing variety of plants. Almost 450 species have been identified on the Gouland Downs, including a number of rarities among the native species. In summer 26 species of orchids and a profusion of native lilies, gentians and daisies contribute a wealth of variety and colour to the tussocklands.

Takahe have been released into the area since 2018 and show signs of becoming established. Although liberated into fairly remote areas some birds have now turned up around the tramper's huts on the Heaphy Track, presumably so that they can scrounge food from the trampers

The descent to the West Coast takes you down through some decidedly 'tropical' country. Tall trees hug the track and a profusion of tree ferns, nikau and smaller plants are to be found and, as a final dramatic contrast, the final stage of the track takes you along the wild West Coast beaches to Karamea.

Other points of interest here are the northernmost breeding colony of fur seals at Wekakura, north of the Heaphy River, and the presence of both long-tailed and short-tailed bats in the park. Kakapo were once common here, particularly in the Upper Karamea and Leslie valleys, but are now gone.

By far the most important area for wildlife in Golden Bay is the wildlife sanctuary on Farewell Spit. Large numbers of waders come here each year, some like the godwits, stints, turnstones and knots from as far away as Siberia. From Collingwood the road takes you over 22 km of winding road to Port Puponga which gives access to the Spit. About halfway down the road leading off to the left will bring you to the Kaihoka Lakes Scenic Reserve on the West Coast which is noted for its huge carnivorous paraphanta snails. Look but don't touch as these are strictly protected.

Gannets (takapu), some of which originally came from White Island in the Bay of Plenty, started nesting on Farewell Spit in 1983 and about 70 nests were built here in their first season. This has now increased to about 9,000 pairs in 4 adjoining groups and the colony is the largest in the South Island – besides being the only one at sea level in New Zealand. This spectacular jump in numbers is attributed to the cessation of pelagic fisheries in Tasman and Golden bays and the consequent increase in surface fish. There are also thousands of waders and about 12,000 black swans. In all there have been 89 bird species recorded from here.

Together with the gannets are nesting colonies of black-backed gulls and Caspian terns, but the white-fronted terns and red-billed gulls that were formerly here have been forced out by the more aggressive gannets.

Farewell Spit is yet another area where whale strandings regularly occur, no doubt because the curve of the bay acts as a natural trap, and every year whales are re-floated from here. Among the whales that have come ashore are minke whales, scamperdown whales and pilot whales. Seven of the twelve strandings of the southern right whale dolphin have also been here. This beautiful dolphin is very distinctive as it lacks a dorsal fin. It is usually found in southern waters but can sometimes be seen on trips out from Kaikoura.

If you are heading south the Nelson Lakes National Park should not be missed. There is easy access to the lakes from Nelson along SH6 to Kawatiri, a distance of around 90 km, an easy drive of a couple of hours. From Kawatiri a further 30 km on SH63 will take you to St Arnaud, the entrance to the park.

This beautiful combination of forests, mountains and lakes has seldom had the attention it deserves. The forests in the lower parts of the park are mainly beech, but miro, kamahi, matai and rimu also occur together with patches of kowhai and rata. The rare orange-fronted parakeet (kakariki karaka) is still found here but in very low numbers. It has now been released on Blumine /Oruawairua Island in the Marlborough Sounds, so there is a faint chance of 'twitching' our rarest land bird on a day trip from Picton. The honeydew secreted by small sap-sucking insects is a vital food source for many birds and lizards but in the past it also attracted many wasps, which competed with the native fauna. These are now rigorously controlled by DoC and although there are still some here, they are at only about 10% of the numbers there once were. Hopefully some sort of biological control will be found and the wasps will eventually be completely eliminated.

Great spotted kiwi (roroa) were moved to this area from the Kahurangi National Park in 2004 and are breeding. Being nocturnal there is not much chance of seeing them but their calls can often be heard at night as these are the most vocal of all kiwi. Their calls carry across the lake and the wharf is a good place to listen for them. During the day the wharf is also a good place to see eels as a number of large and fairly tame individuals hang out there. Once again I suspect some sort of inducement is involved.

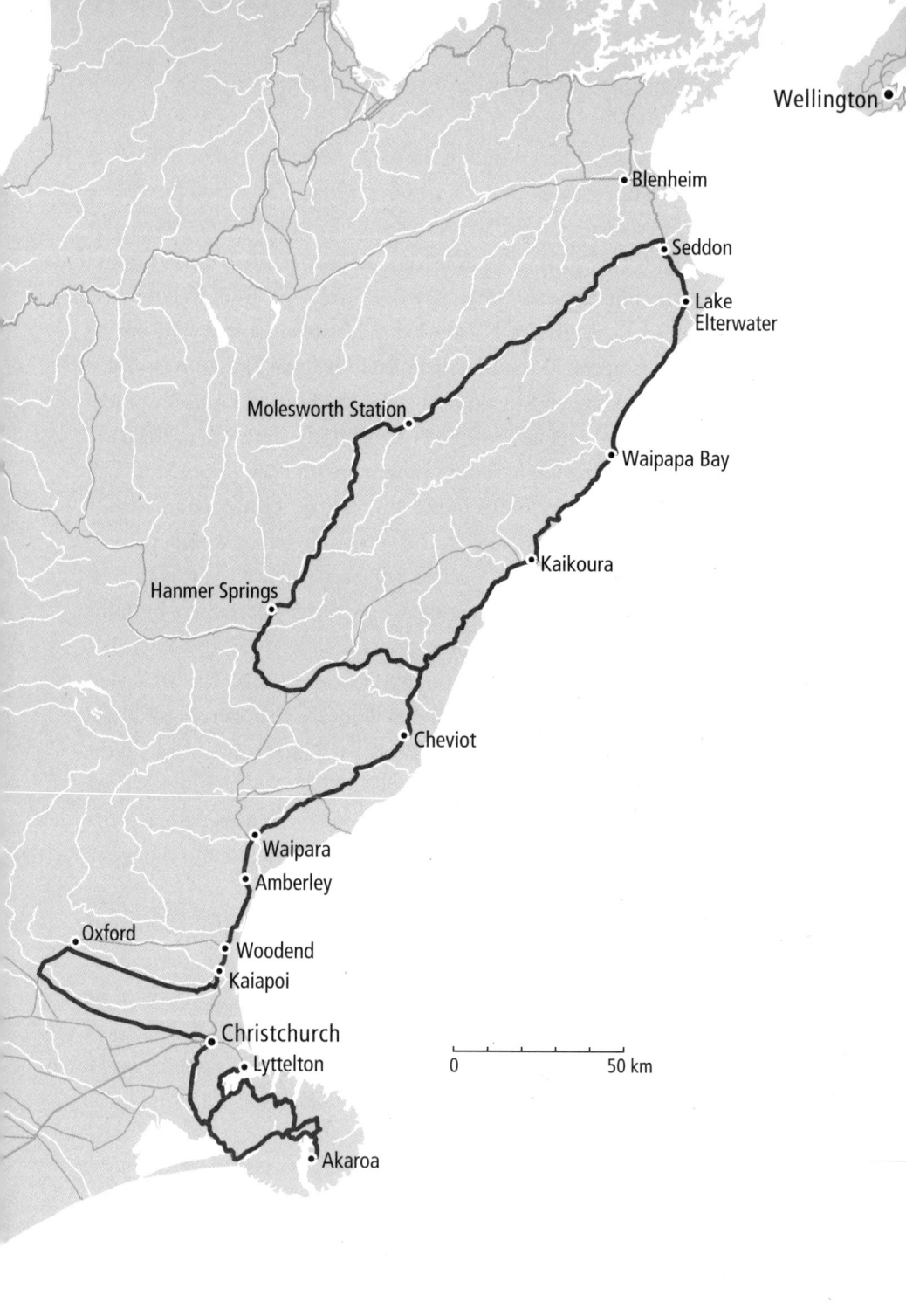

CHAPTER 11

Kaikoura and Canterbury/Waitaha

Starting about twenty five million years ago, this region was the site of New Zealand's most recent period of sustained mountain building. The name given to that great epoch is the Kaikoura Orogeny, named for the mountains it created. Even today the mountains of Kaikoura are still rising as the ranges along this area's faults move northwards. This has at times resulted in severe earthquakes in the region, causing large scale damage. In 2016 a 7.8mw earthquake, deposited nearly a million metres of rock and material onto SH1 both north and south of Kaikoura resulting in a huge amount of damage which has taken a number of years to fully repair. The earthquake affected both the shoreline and the sea life.

From the sea as you look inland, the mountains seem to rise in a continuous mass to the horizon, but in fact there are two parallel ranges – the Seaward and the Inland Kaikouras – divided by a deep fault. Through part of that fault runs the Clarence River, reaching the Pacific 7 km north of Waipapa Bay.

It is the Seaward Kaikouras that dominate the landscape along the coast as the route from Blenheim via SH1 heads first south-east and then almost directly south. It is just short of 130 km to Kaikoura and for almost half this distance the Pacific is within sight of the road. Even if you allow time for sightseeing, this trip can still be done easily within three hours.

Squeezed between the mountains and the sea, the plain here often narrows to a strip just metres wide or disappears entirely. Then the road and the railway enter tunnels laboriously carved into the coastal cliffs. Nowhere else in New Zealand do mountains run so closely parallel to the sea and there is nowhere else on the mainland that the sea exerts such an influence on the environment as it does in the coastal Kaikoura region. Living on the roadside cliffs there are a number of interesting insects which include some fascinating weta. These include one of the most distinctive members of the group, the Kaikoura giant weta, *Deinacrida parva,* plus a number of interesting cave wetas including the most striking of this group, the aptly named elegant cave weta, *Pleioplectron rodmorrisi,* named for one of our leading nature photographers.

Stop at any of the numerous nooks and crannies along this coast, walk down to the beach and one can observe the abundant sea life the shore supports. The sea here is often rough and breakers crash against a rock-bound shore cushioned only slightly by the giant kelp writhing in slow motion in the current. This kelp, (rimurapa) *Durvillea antarctica,* with its firm holdfast, smooth blades and dark, sinuous thongs offers minimum resistance to the waves and so is superbly adapted to this environment and grows much larger here than it does in the north.

There is an amazing variety of life all along this exposed, seemingly hostile shore. Every tidepool supports its own tiny community of fish, crabs, starfish and other invertebrates. *Lithothamnia* spp. algae cover the rocks in splashes of greens, mauves and pinks and periwinkles range widely throughout the splash zone grazing on algae. Scarlet, chocolate and orange sponges and sometimes the gently waving antennae of crayfish can be seen deep in the water-filled crevices, together with green mussels and barnacles firmly attached to the rocks.

This abundant 'kai moana' was greatly appreciated by Maori who migrated from the north. Most modern translations of Kaikoura are given as 'eat crayfish', but Kaikoura is actually a shortened version of the original name, Te-Ahi-Kai-Koura-a-Tamatea-Pokai-Whenua, meaning the fire at which crayfish were cooked for Tamatea-Pokai-Whenua, the legendary explorer. The local Ngati Rangitane also trolled for barracouta in the surrounding seas and fished for the blue cod, parrotfish and spotties which favour these rocky coasts.

Whales are a feature of the Kaikoura coast and, although the migrating pods of yesteryear are now much diminished, they are still to be seen. Tours to view the whales can be taken but are, of course, weather dependant. Sperm whales are the main species seen but there are a number of other cetaceans and a host of seabirds. Some sperm whales (paraoa) migrate here each year but there are young bulls resident year round. Orca (kera wera) often occur too and Hector's dolphin can usually be found closer inshore.

Seabirds, (as mentioned) are another highlight of the boat tours. Masses of petrels can be seen and albatrosses are not unusual around here, on forays from the south. Several dozen different procellariids frequent our waters, some in great numbers but others only rarely, and it is worthwhile learning to differentiate between the various types. Some of these birds formerly occurred in huge numbers.

Captain Waller of the ship *Westralia*, crossing the Tasman at the turn of the 20th century, reported that on one occasion he steamed for 50 km through flights of 'muttonbirds' and these extended for more than 5 km on either side of the ship. When the birds settled on the sea to feed he likened them to a reef of black rocks. Giant petrels or stinkpots are also common and the leg and wing bones of these birds were used by Maori for the making of needles and awls. Watch out for penguins too. They have abysmal road sense.

The fur seal is only now making a comeback in this area after the onslaught of the sealers in the first few decades of the 19th century. Hundreds of thousands were killed in our southern waters to cater for the European pelt trade before legal protection was brought in early last century. Now, once again, they are found along the Kaikoura coast in large numbers and fishermen are asking that legal protection be removed because the seals compete with them for fish.

Around Kaikoura town there is plenty to see and do. Take the road to the beacon on Point Keane at the road's end about 1.5 km east of the town. This takes you past pocket-sized sandy beaches, large areas of rugged rocks and a tiny lagoon. At low tide, the many exposed sand patches and rocky pools provide good pickings for herons, shags and waders. White-faced herons stalk up and down in their pedantic manner: golden plovers, godwits, turnstones and other waders quarter the exposed sand, while at the lagoon there is usually a resident pair of paradise shelduck together with mallards, pied stilts and dotterels.

In spring the rocks opposite Point Keane bustle with the comings and goings of the thousands of nesting red-billed and black-backed gulls and white-fronted terns. Fur seals also haul out on the rocks in large numbers in the winter and there are usually a few bachelor bulls to be seen most times of the year.

Two kilometres south from Kaikoura on SH1 are the Maori Leap Caves – limestone caverns carved from the cliffs by subterranean streams. These are noted for their stalactites and stalagmites but also contain fossilised bones of penguins and seals. Also near Kaikoura is one of the two known mainland colonies of a giant weta, the Kaikoura giant weta, *Deinacrida parva*, and one of the most attractive of our endemic plants, a native tree broom, *Chordospartium stevensonii*, found now in only a few localities, one being in coastal gullies north of Kaikoura.

The ranges inland are worth exploring and can be reached by taking the road north from Hanmer Springs, which is 140 km south-west of Kaikoura, off SH70. Hanmer Springs is a small resort town and the last settlement so if you are taking the road north stock up here. From Hanmer the road moves into the Awatere River Valley just past Molesworth Station and will eventually bring you out again on the coast just north of Seddon, 137 km from Hanmer. This road is difficult and can be blocked by snow in winter so check before venturing onto it.

Molesworth station is huge comprising of 180,000 ha of Crown land made up of several sheep stations that were resumed and amalgamated by the government in the 1930s. At the time of this resumption the whole area was in very poor condition because of overgrazing by sheep and infestation by rabbits. Pasture improvement and pest control has since benefited this area greatly.

Around Molesworth Station is a vast expanse of tussock and grassland, picturesquely set between the Inland Kaikouras and the Spenser Mountains. Among its highlights are the mountain valleys of the Waiau, Clarence, Rainbow and Wairau rivers with their mixture of beech forests and tussocklands. Lake Tennyson, set like a deep blue sapphire among the golden tussock and moraine wetlands, is also worth visiting.

From Molesworth north the road for almost its entire distance runs alongside the Awatere River at the foot of the Inland Kaikouras. Contrary

to first appearances these mountains support a wide variety of life. Vegetable sheep (tutahuna) abound at the higher altitudes and from a distance it is easy to see how these white and woolly plants get their name. Much less common is *Hebe ramossissima*, a small shrub, which has been collected from only three sites in the Kaikouras.

One of the most recent reptile discoveries in New Zealand was a nocturnal gecko, collected in the Inland Kaikouras. This lives among the tussock and scrub in rocky, alpine areas and is now called the Black-eyed Gecko, *Mokopirirakau kahutarae*.

The Inland Kaikouras rise to an impressive 2,700 m and run into the Blue Mountain Range in the north. This, too, is bleak and seemingly inhospitable country. Much of the country lies under snow from April to October and in summer the grass always looks parched. Nevertheless, here and there are isolated farmhouses. These homesteads, usually huddled among small groups of exotic trees, look small and vulnerable at the foot of the high mountains or tucked away at the bottom of huge valleys.

Here at Lake Elterwater not far out of Ward one of our latest avian arrivals the hoary-headed grebe (taihoropi) has settled and is now breeding, but a number of other waterbirds can also be easily seen including scaup and this is one of the most likely places to see one of our rarest natives, the Chestnut-breasted shelduck.

Back at Kaikoura township, travel south along SH1. The hills now are much reduced after the soaring peaks behind Kaikoura and it is not until you reach Omihi, some 111 km further south, that the Canterbury Plains open out before you. This wide expanse is the country's most distinctive and easily defined geographical area – by far the largest, contiguous area of lowland we have.

This long, coastal plain is flanked on the west by the soaring peaks of the Southern Alps and from these to the coast run the great rivers of the plains – the Waimakariri, Rakaia and the Rangitata – all running eastward to the sea.

Geologists estimate that less than a million years ago the waters of the Pacific Ocean lapped right up to the base of these mountains, but slowly, by glaciation, and by the action of the rivers, the mountains were eroded and the debris in the form of gravel carried down to the sea. These coarse gravels were deposited at the river mouths in great fan-like deposits pushing simultaneously seaward and sideward to eventually join up and form the plains. At the intersections of these deposits, smaller rivers such as the Ashley, the Selwyn and the Ashburton now flow.

These deposited gravels reach depths of up to a kilometre, while the soil cover is comparatively thin (on average 20 to 25 cm) and often fragile, mostly made up of loess but also with some alluvial patches near the rivers.

Early settlers thought the Canterbury Plains had always been grass covered but research now indicates that almost this entire area was covered with totara-dominated forest up to about 2,000 years ago. Then huge fires devastated many areas, but particularly those along the drier, eastern coast of both islands. The most affected areas were in the MacKenzie Basin and Central Otago but also, to a lesser degree, South Canterbury.

After the arrival of Maori much of the remaining forest of the Canterbury Plains was burnt. Why this was done can only remain a matter for speculation. Explanations include clearing the land for agriculture and building, providing conditions for bracken to flourish (for the edible fern root) or to facilitate cross-country travel but none of these alone could account for the sheer magnitude of the burning that was done. The only reasonable explanation is that once fires were lit in these drier eastern regions they soon got out of control and very large areas were burnt.

South of Omihi, an exquisitely exact pattern of paddocks stretches south as far as the eye can see and west to the foothills of the Southern Alps, which dominate the landscape of much of the South Island. You can best appreciate this scenery from the air in spring or summer when the variety of crops create a vast checkerboard of varying colours, but good views can also be had from hill lookouts such as those on Banks Peninsula.

One of the most persistent features of the Canterbury Plains is its braided rivers. These are formed by the deposit of wide expanses of shingle which originate as rock debris eroded from the mountains. Large rivers cut through this accumulated shingle and their constantly changing courses have created riverbeds over a kilometre wide in some places. When crossing rivers such as the Rakaia by train one wonders when the bridge will end.

No native trees grow here, but there are a number of shrubs such as the thorny wild Irishman and several *Hebe* and *Epilobium* species. More typical are the scabweeds which form dense and often colourful mats. The common scabweed *Raoulia australis,* forms greenish-grey patches over a metre wide and mossy scabweed is found in attractive golden moss-like colonies.

The birds of these areas are unique too. Wrybills, black-fronted terns, South Island pied oystercatchers, black-billed gulls, banded dotterels and the very rare black stilt are all braided riverbed breeders and the wrybill breeds nowhere else. The birds return each spring and after their chicks fledge generally move to the coast or migrate northwards with some of the banded dotterels even wintering in Australia.

A classic example of a braided river is the Waimakariri River and this is easily reached by taking the road running alongside it, a couple of kilometres past Kaiapoi. Large numbers of black-backed gulls nest and roost along the Waimakariri, sallying forth each morning and at dusk in search of food. Many make for the surrounding farmlands but some travel daily as far afield as Lyttelton Harbour, a round trip of well over 100 km. However, these gulls are a major predator of other river nesters and will need controlling.

From the Waimakariri River it is a short drive into Christchurch. If Canterbury is the most European of our landscapes, Christchurch is certainly the most English of our cities. Arriving on the treeless plains around the Avon, the mostly English immigrants immediately set out to recreate a replica of home. Walk the streets of Christchurch today, wander through the square with its London planes, or sit under the willows along the Avon and share your lunch with the ducks and you could very well be by the original river in England – except for the swans being black, not white.

Planting of exotic trees started early here. The Deans brothers, who settled at Riccarton in 1843, started importing trees almost immediately, as did the French at nearby Akaroa. Tree planting tended to follow trends, as one of our earlier amateur naturalists, Thomas Henry Potts, noted. Although he arrived in Canterbury in 1854, a mere 15 years after Pakeha settlement had commenced, he observed:

> There is a fashion for planting trees as in other matters; old settlers can doubtless recollect the rise, progress, and decay of the willow and poplar period, which was succeeded by a furor for the blue gum Eucalyptus globulus, this stately, fast-growing Australasian in its turn had to succumb to the fresher attractions of the Californian coniferae of whose economic uses but little that is certain is yet known. How long will the needle-leaved pines hold their own on public favour?'

With the settlers came a huge increase in the number of insect pests. In 1860 W.L.T. Travers published a paper called 'The Bird As the Labourer of Man' and described:

> ...the extraordinary clouds of moths of all kinds which arose from the ground as one walked, either through the tussock-covered areas or through fields of cultivated grass. In the Rangiora district trenches were often dug to intercept millions of caterpillar when marching towards growing crops, and the ravages they committed where no means of protection existed were very serious.

It was partly to provide this means of protection that the Canterbury Acclimatisation Society was formed in 1864. The gentlemen of the society promptly imported a large number of birds, which included among others sparrows. In later years when suggestions were made that this had been a less than inspired choice the Society, along with most other societies throughout the country, hastily denied responsibility.

They also denied having any part in the introduction of the rabbit (rapeti), which soon became a major pest in Canterbury. The first to be brought in were carefully protected and a Captain Ruck Keene who farmed near Kaikoura sacked two of his employees for shooting at rabbits recently liberated on his property. Shortly before the rabbits ate him into bankruptcy he said he should have rewarded the men and trained them to be better shots. The rabbits spread with lightning speed, giving rise to a wry observation by farmers on what they called 'rabbit arithmetic' – that two times three equals nine million, this being the possible progeny of two rabbits over three years.

From Christchurch one of the better trips is around Banks Peninsula. Banks Peninsula is made up of the remnants of two basaltic volcanoes, Lyttleton and Akaroa, which became extinct about 5.5 million years ago. Until the recent geological past this area was an island, but was joined to the mainland by the gradual eastward movement of the Canterbury Plains. Cook thought that Banks Peninsula was an island when he sailed past, but at this time it was already part of the mainland.

While in the city make a stop at Riccarton or Deans Bush, three kilometres west of Cathedral Square, along Riccarton Road. This is the only remnant today of the swamp forest which once flourished around Christchurch and good examples can be seen here of totara, matai, kahikatea and rata together with a good selection of regenerating growth.

From Riccarton take SH75 through Taitapu and Motukarara to the north-east corner of Lake Ellesmere/Te Waihora at Birdlings Flat, from where a detour to the lake is recommended. Its actual size varies considerably, depending on such factors as tides and inflow, ranging from some 20,000 ha to almost 24,000 ha.

In keeping with its size Lake Ellesmere is home to our largest population of Canada geese, and black and white swans are found here along with countless ducks and waders. Some 158 species have been recorded at Ellesmere, of which 80 are regular users. The lake is also home to our largest colony of mute swans.

One of the names local Ngai Tahu gave the lake was Te Kete Ika a Rakaihautu, 'the fish basket of Rakaihautu'. They used the reeds and flax for weaving, the waters for transport and the mud for dyes. More importantly, as the kumara was at its southern limit and thus probably a marginal crop, they relied on the lake for much of their food, catching large numbers of eels, flounder and other fish.

From Ellesmere continue on around the Peninsula to the French settlement of Akaroa on Akaroa Harbour. In the harbour Hector's dolphin can often be found – it has the unenviable title of being one of the world's rarest marine dolphin. Being an inshore species it is especially vulnerable to being caught in set nets. In an effort to protect it some 14,310 sq. km around the peninsula have been declared a sanctuary.

The white-flippered penguin also occurs around Banks Peninsula. Opinion is divided as to whether this is a full species or merely a sub species of the little blue penguin. After breeding it disperses to feeding grounds elsewhere and young birds have been found as far north as East Cape and as far south as Otago. Another bird worth watching for is the spotted shag, which breeds in crevices in the cliffs.

From Akaroa take the road back to Christchurch via Pigeon Bay and Ohinetahi. Few sizeable areas of standing timber remain on Banks Peninsula, but what there is is mainly in reserves, some of it around Pigeon Bay.

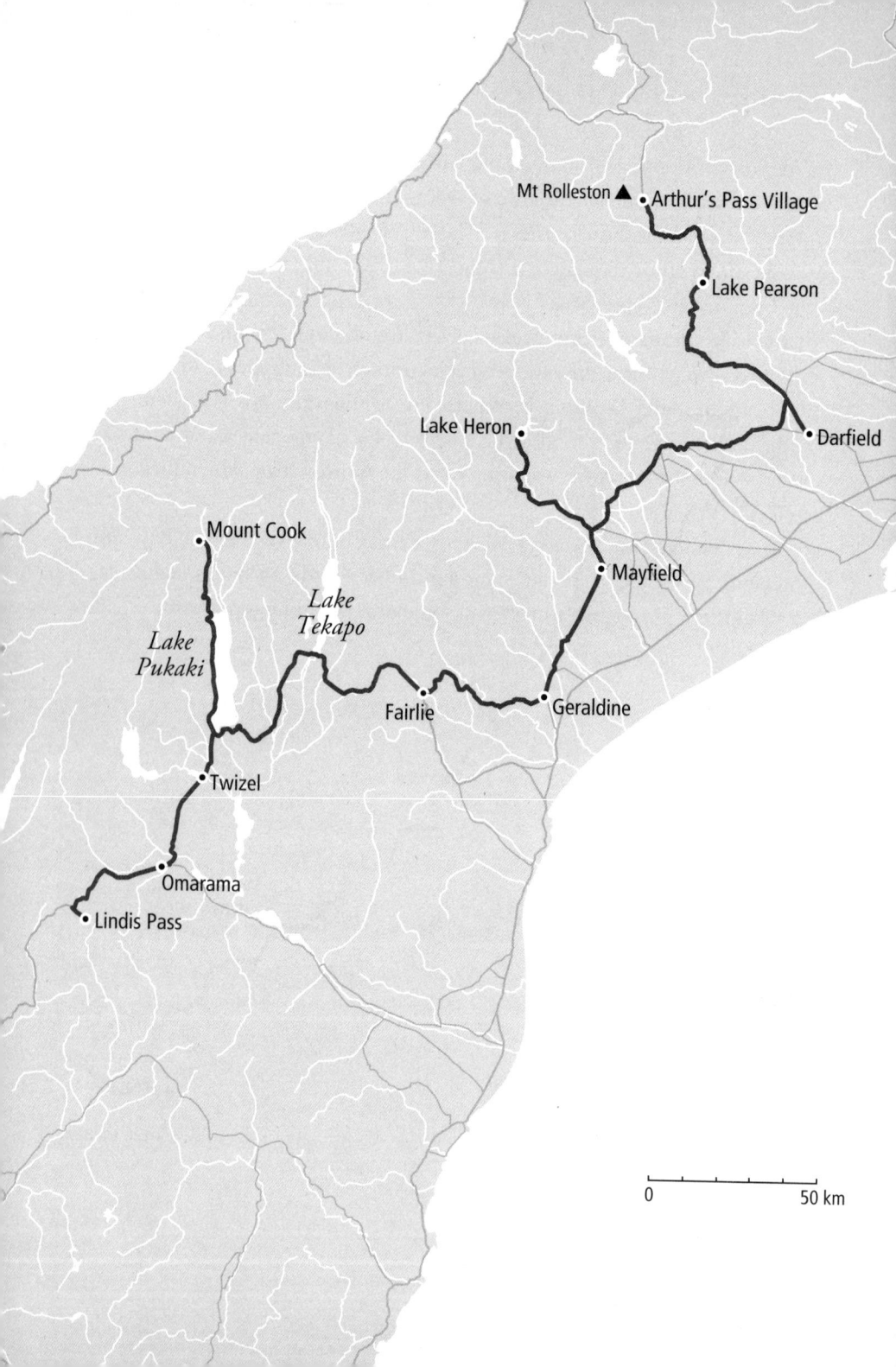

CHAPTER 12

The Southern Alps/Te Tiritiri-o-te-moana

Following European settlement, it was sheepmen who first explored the mountain wilderness of the Southern Alps in their search for grazing lands beyond the Canterbury Plains, but gold prospectors opened it up. Gold was first discovered on the West Coast in 1863 and gold seekers attracted by the prospects of a quick fortune, trekked in their droves from Canterbury through the rugged mountains. They crossed the Alps by way of Harper Pass but the constant traffic of gold seekers and stock turned the track into a muddy, boulder-strewn mess and finding an alternative route became imperative.

In February 1864 Arthur Dobson and his brother Edward rode up the Waimakariri River and up the Bealey Valley. From there they travelled across the bed of an old glacier to the West Coast. Because of the steep descent on the western side Arthur was not too enthusiastic about the route, declaring that it was difficult, if not impossible. His father, who was Canterbury's regional engineer, decided otherwise, and 1,000 men were put to work building a road. Using rudimentary tools and labouring through the harsh alpine winter, they built the road to the West Coast in less than a year. The result today is the highest and most spectacular of our alpine highways which opened in March 1866 and it is from Arthur's Pass this road trip commences.

Around Arthur's Pass itself, there is much to see. The Bealey Valley is rich in birdlife below and above the tree line. This includes kereru, kea and kakariki and the great spotted kiwi, or roroa. Most evenings they can be heard calling up the valley. If you are lucky you may see the rock wren bobbing around among the boulders and the blue duck in the streams. Kea are especially active when the mountain flax (wharariki) is in flower and there is a very small chance of seeing kakariki karaka. Ask at the DoC office.

For flower fanciers the best time to visit Arthur's Pass is between November and late February. There are several specialities in the area which the park rangers will advise you of and every few years the Otira Gorge is ablaze with flowering rata. Keep an eye out for the aptly named Horrid Spaniard, *Aciphylla horrida*, and the only slightly less horrid Wild Spaniard *A. colensoi (taramea)*.

When driving between Westland and Christchurch on SH73 one passes by way of Flock Hill then Castle Hill to Porters Pass, the final pass on the West Coast–Christchurch road. Although Arthur's Pass is better known, Porters Pass at 945.5 m is actually 14 m higher. From this Pass great views can be had over the Canterbury Plains, a panorama which gold seekers returning from the West Coast must have gazed upon with considerable relief. Today Porters Pass is a popular ski resort as it is within relatively easy driving of Christchurch. Nearby Lake Lyndon is popular too, with skaters, being one of the few South Island lakes which sometimes fully freezes over.

The lakes in the Southern Alps, however, are mostly too deep and cold to support much birdlife and those birds that are here frequent sheltered, shallow areas. In summer a number of birds come here to nest, including the nattily dressed South Island pied oystercatchers, with their distinctive black and white plumage nicely set off by a scarlet beak. Although usually found nesting along riverbeds on the plains, they not infrequently use the lake shore. Also nesting at the lakeside is the banded dotterel. This bird was called tuturiwhatu by Maori because of the trilling call of the male when courting.

Across Lake Lyndon to the west Mount Lyndon can be seen and to the north-east rise the rugged Torlesse Ranges. These were explored by the surveyor Charles Torlesse in 1849 who aptly described them as a *romantic and chaotic mass of mountains*.

This area was the realm of the buff weka which was regularly snared by Maori when crossing the Alps seeking greenstone on the West Coast. However, weka learned to avoid the snares, giving rise to the Maori proverb: 'Makere te weka i te mahanga e hoki ano' for which a very rough translation would be 'once bitten, twice shy'.

The buff weka disappeared in the 1920s, perhaps for the same reasons which caused it to die out in the north – predators and possibly diseases transmitted by poultry. Fortunately for the weka, if not for the local Rekohu birds, it had been introduced earlier to the Chatham Islands from where it has now been reintroduced to Arthur's Pass National Park as well as onto islands on Lakes Wanaka and Wakatipu.

Nearby Castle Hill/Kura Tawhiti has a number of cave drawings and these are said to be about 500 years old and are drawn with a mixture of fat and charcoal.

Castle Hill is also known for its flowers. Here a number of plants have adapted to the limestone 'moonscape' of the periglacial zone and some of the best of these are natives. Best known among them is the endemic Castle Hill buttercup, *Ranunculus paucifolius* – a spectacular plant with large golden flowers growing on shortened stems among brown-green leaves. This plant is one of our rarest plants and is particularly threatened by the grazing of hares (hea).

To the west of Castle Hill is the Craigieburn Range and, as in all other parts of the Southern Alps, the surrounding tree cover is beech – mountain beech predominating but with patches of silver and red. Around the 1,100 m mark this gives way to subalpine scrub but the speciality of the region is its alpine plants.

Beyond the Craigieburn there is little cover. Much of the land was devastated by early settlers burning off the tussock to create grazing for their sheep. This resulted in scree and shingle slipping off the hillsides into the valleys and riverbeds below and much of this material has ended up in Lake Pearson. The lake today is completely surrounded by eroded hills and although the Forest Service is in the process of replanting these hills, the job is immense.

The lake itself contains rainbow and brown trout and one of our rarest waterfowl, the beautiful crested grebe (puteketeke). It is the most aquatic of our birds, its legs being set so far back on its body that it can neither stand nor walk on land and so it must live, breed and nest on the water. This bird has gone into a steep decline in recent years and now numbers only about 1,000 birds. This has been caused by predators, hunting and probably by being disturbed by boaties. Where these threats are mitigated these birds are thriving and motorised boats are now banned on Lake Pearson.

Other grebes to be found in these lakes are the Australian little grebe (tokitokipio) and the hoary-headed grebe (tohoropi), also known as Tom Pudding. Both are rare vagrants from Australia but there are hopeful signs that they will become established here and breeding has been noted in several areas.

From Porters Pass travel through Springfield onto the Canterbury Plains, and turn right at Darfield onto SH77 along the foothills of the spectacular alps. This highway eventually comes out on the Rakaia, one of the largest of the braided rivers. Near here Thomas Potts spent some time exploring and in April 1856 he found the South Island kokako still plentiful along the banks of the Rakaia writing *under favourable conditions the kokako may be found on the outskirts of the bush, in the open glades that fringe some of the larger rivers. The gentle confident manners, the rich flute-like notes, the peculiar mode of progression even, cannot fail to draw the attention of the observer.*

The piopio, which vanished even faster than the kokako, was another favourite of Potts and was then still plentiful around here. Most early observers noted how forward it was. For Potts the piopio was *as bold as the robin or tit without their intrusive friendliness.*

From the charmingly named town of Windwhistle you might like to follow the road north-west along the Rakaia to Lake Coleridge, but because the lake is too deep and cold to support much birdlife a better proposition is probably the Ashburton Lakes, which lie south of the Rakaia and can be reached by following the road up the Ashburton River from Mt Somers. These lakes lie on the bottom of glaciated basins and hence they are shallow and better suited to waterfowl.

They are also surrounded by extensive wetlands and areas of red tussock, bog rush and carex, which makes them attractive to swamp dwellers such as the bittern (matuku hurepo), the marsh crake (koitareke) and the spotless crake (puweto). Best known of these is Lake Heron and although its namesake the kotuku, or white heron, is now a rare visitor, 20 other species of waterfowl can also be found here, including the crested grebe, the dapper scaup and

other ducks, along with the coot which has recently migrated into this area.

Not so popular with the farmers who live in this area are the large numbers of Canada geese (kuihi) which nest around the lakes and fly out to feed in the surrounding farmlands, grazing on the pasture and fouling the paddocks. Also found here is another introduction, the chukar partridge. About 15 pairs of chukar were liberated in the Lake Heron district in 1926 and the following year a further 25 birds were released near Lake Hawea. Different races, one from Persia (now Iran), and the other from the Himalayas, were released at the opposite ends of the Alps and so far these seem to be breeding true. They are regularly seen around Aoraki/Mt Cook and at the Mt John Observatory near Tekapo.

From Lake Heron we travel south and at Arundel on the Rangitata River there is a turnoff to Erewhon Station where the author Samuel Butler farmed from 1860 to 1864. His book *A First Year in Canterbury Settlement* is well worth reading for the insight it provides into early colonial life.

From Arundel, the road continues across the plains to Geraldine on SH79. After passing through foothills now being turned into yet another pine forest the road descends into Beautiful Valley, followed quickly by Cattle Valley and then Fairlie. It then travels along the foothills of the Two Thumb Range, all stock-raising land, into the MacKenzie Country. With so many place names glorifying politicians and businesspeople it makes a change to find a place named for a sheep thief. Britain has its Robin Hood and Australia its Ned Kelly, and we have our James MacKenzie, with his rather innovative method of training his dog to help him rustle sheep.

The MacKenzie Country is made up of the drainage basins of Lakes Tekapo, Pukaki and Ohau as well as the tributaries of the Upper Waitaki and covers more than 16,000 ha of land, once all in tussock. It has a few claims to fame: a giant weta, a newly described scree weta, and an endemic butterfly, the southern blue. This is in danger of being hybridised into extinction by a recent Australian immigrant, the common blue, and as such is seemingly destined for the same fate as the black stilt.

The black stilt (kaki), was once our most common stilt, but predation, combined with the opening up of the country which better suited its relative the pied stilt (poaka), has meant a sharp drop in numbers. This decline has forced the black stilt to take pied stilts as mates, resulting in an increasing number of hybrids called 'smudgies' and today not many pure kaki survive. At last count I think it was 169 adults.

Nesting enclosures for the black stilt have been built by the Forest and Bird Society near Lake Tekapo to keep out predators and black stilt eggs are being given to pied stilts for fostering. However, this has led to some behaviour changes by the fostered chicks, which may reduce the effectiveness of the foster care programme: these black stilts now migrate north with their foster parents instead of wintering in the MacKenzie Country with other black stilts and frequent the Kawhia and Aotea harbours.

Parallel to Lake Tekapo is Lake Pukaki and by following the shores of this lake you arrive at Mt Cook/Aoraki, our highest mountain and centre of probably our best known national park, the Aoraki/Mt Cook National Park. On a clear day the drive up to Aoraki/Mt Cook is breathtaking, with the huge mass of the mountain dominating the landscape. Although the view from any direction is tremendous my favourite is across Lake Pukaki, with the mountain soaring above the vivid, turquoise waters of the lake.

Aoraki/Mt Cook is a good place to stay for a couple of days while exploring the park but make sure it is not in the skiing season. Then you stand a good chance of being skittled by a skier while watching birds and, anyway, all the interesting plants are under several metres of snow.

At this height above sea level all the birds, except the kea and the rock wren, spend the winter at lower altitudes where the pickings are presumably better, but in summer migrate back to the higher reaches. Paradise shelducks and harriers can both be seen around the park in summer together with black-backed gulls and pipits. Even pukeko stray up from time to time and look very much out of place in the snowfields.

The monarch of the mountains is undoubtedly the kea. He struts around with a proprietorial air, sticking his beak into anything left unguarded. Heaven help the campers who go off and leave their packs or tent unattended.

Its sabre-like beak is not ornamental and even windscreen wiper rubbers, the roofs of convertible cars and motorbike seats are an easy target for a kea with its heart set on mischief.

Department of Conservation staff at tourist resorts have recently begun a campaign to discourage travellers from feeding kea in the hope that they will move away from settled areas and start foraging for themselves again.

But despite their failings, kea have a raffish charm shared by few other birds. The late British Naturalist Gerald Durrell, was much taken with them on a visit to Mt Cook. He was particularly taken by *their strutting pompous walk, their general attitude of being lords of all they surveyed, combined with their (oft) repeated and never varying cry.* From a distance their plumage appears a drab olive colour but close up it reveals a marvellous range of russet shades with the orange undersides of their wings glowing like flashes of flame.

Around the Mt Cook environs are other animals that, like the kea, are not universally popular: the chamois and the thar. In 1904 the Duke of Bedford sent six Himalayan thar from his herd at Woburn, in England, which were liberated at Mt Cook and these were followed by three other liberations. Eight chamois arrived at Mt Cook as a gift from the Emperor of Austria in 1907 with a further two in 1914.

Both have thrived and spread over a great part of the Southern Alps. Hunting pressure on these animals is considerable. Well over 100,000 thar have been killed by private and government hunters since protection was removed in 1930, but this has only slightly checked their numbers and in the meantime the damage they do to alpine vegetation is calamitous. Not only is much of this vegetation unique, but its removal is worsening an already serious erosion problem. Unfortunately, the removal of the animals entirely is almost impossible and, even if it were not, pressure from hunting interests would probably prevent it.

However, the vegetation around Mt Cook is particularly good as browsing animals are more easily kept under control here. The Mount Cook buttercup (formerly known as the Mount Cook lily) is the world's largest buttercup, is well known and deservedly acclaimed, but there are also many other plants which, even if not quite as spectacular, are beautiful and worth seeking out. Among these are the large mountain daisy, or tikumu, the alpine buttercup, the snow gentian, the New Zealand eyebright (tutumako), and the various marguerites and bluebells. Some people have commented that our alpine flora are mostly all white or yellow, lacking the range of colours of mountain flowers in other countries. I personally think that quite a few, particularly the daises and buttercups, are superb.

The tikumu was prized by early Maori, as the pellicles of the leaves were plaited into headbands and the white soft wool used as hair ornaments. The stiff, spiny leaves of the speargrass were also valued as a source of aromatic gums for use in scented oils.

From Aoraki/Mt Cook travel along SH80 and SH8 via Twizel to the Lindis Pass. On the frequent cold, clear days of this part of the South Island, the Pass offers magnificent views and links the alpine scenery of the MacKenzie Country with the varied splendour of Central Otago and there can be very few places in the world where such a wide range of dramatically different landscapes can be encountered in such a relatively small area.

CHAPTER 13

Southland and Otago – Murihiku and Otakou.

From the MacKenzie Country we travel over the Lindis Pass to Central Otago. From Omarama, SH8 follows the Ahuriri River and turns south up Longslip Creek to reach the pass. It was long familiar to pre-European Maori who passed here on their way to the West Coast seeking greenstone. Otago surveyor John Turnbull Thomson named the area after the island of Lindisfarne off the coast of Northumberland in the United Kingdom.

The view from the Pass is remarkable with tussock-covered mountains stretching off into the vast distances. There is little in the way of larger vegetation apart from a few patches of matagouri and sweet briar and some willows along the stream. Otherwise, everywhere there is tussock. Considering the amount of tussockland that is to be found throughout Otago, Canterbury and the Southern Alps, it has received extremely little recognition as a distinct and valuable ecosystem. Until quite recently less than 10 ha of more than a million in the Otago area had reserve status.

There are few birds either. By leaving the road and remaining quiet you may see the lovely chukar. The scarce falcon, or karearea, can also sometimes be seen, its piercing whistle or scream often betraying its presence before it comes into sight. Pipits are particularly common and these are the main prey of the falcon together with an occasional young rabbit. The harrier is also found here and it feeds on rabbits as well.

About 15 km south of the Pass is Morven Hills Station. This was one of the largest stations in the South Island, covering some 161,844 ha and was started around 1859 by the brothers John and Allan McLean. By 1874, when they sold it, they had built their flock to an impressive 135,154 sheep.

Near the summit is a plaque commemorating the release in this area of seven red deer which had been imported from Scotland. From Morven Hills they spread in all directions with devastating results. But these were not the only deer liberated in the province: in 1867 axis deer were brought from Melbourne and released at Bushy Park but proved such a nuisance by raiding crops that they were shot by local farmers. Fallow deer were the next to arrive and had better luck, being released in the Tapanui Hills from where they have spread widely.

From the summit follow the road alongside the Clutha River to Cromwell and thence to Clyde, Alexandra and Roxburgh. The Clutha is fed by the three lakes — Wakatipu, Wanaka and Hawea — which contribute to the Clutha's flow of 650 cubic metres per second (cusecs), the largest flow rate in the country. In its higher reaches near Lake Wanaka it is a favoured spot with anglers for its rainbow and brown trout.

Cromwell is picturesque and set on a promontory at the confluence of the Kawarau and Clutha Rivers, but much of the older part of the town has disappeared beneath the waters of the dam that was built near Clyde. In preparation for the extensive flooding, archaeologists had for several years been exploring the area around Cromwell and discovered, among other things, a number of moa-hunter sites — suggesting that this area once sustained sizeable moa populations.

An earlier archaeological find near the Clutha in 1892, and now in the Otago Museum, was a waka huia, or carved box of huia feathers. While sheltering in a cave near Talla Burn, on the opposite side of the Clutha from Rae's Junction, George Rae saw what he thought was a piece of sacking in a dry crevice. On closer examination this turned out to be the waka huia, which contained, as well as 70 huia feathers, 20 bunches of scarlet kaka feathers. It has been suggested they were brought from the north to be used in exchange for greenstone.

Near Cromwell lives one of our rarest known insects, the Cromwell chafer beetle, *Prodontria lewisii,* which is confined to an 81 ha fenced reserve near the town. It is not a particularly impressive looking insect and although it does not get the recognition of our larger endangered species like dolphins and birds it deserves protection notwithstanding. The Cromwell Borough Council once proposed building a rubbish dump near the reserve but it was feared that the seagulls and rats that such dumps attract could endanger the beetles, so this proposal was shelved.

Most of this area was once a hive of activity as thousands of miners worked their claims. Large volumes of gold were extracted with large amounts of earth and rock being moved to get at it so many of the scars are still visible today. The most recent tailings are white, devoid of vegetation, but the older areas are gradually being covered by adventive scrub and willows.

When Maori arrived here in the Maniototo, there were great forests of tremendous diversity in Central Otago, but in the first few centuries of settlement most of this was burnt. A great deal of the vegetation that is to be seen here now is exotic and in autumn this provides a blaze of colour.

The climate of Central Otago has been compared to that of central California and trees from that area do particularly well here. Monterey pine, *Pinus radiata,* and bull pine, *P. ponderosa,* and big-cone pines, (whose cones are the size of basketballs) and *P. coulteri,* all thrive and the occasional California big tree is also to be found. Unfortunately some of the pines have thrived too well and seeds spreading throughout the high country have resulted in wilding pines, which have covered hundreds of thousands of hectares of DoC land.

The climate is also suitable for horticulture and when the gold ran out many miners turned their hands to orchards. Today Central Otago is the centre for much of our stonefruit industry. Grapes are also grown and these date from an early French settler, Jean Feraud, who produced some of the first wine in the south. Alexandra, 31 km south-east of Cromwell, is a fruit-growing area and the trees form an oasis in what has been called the 'dry core' of Otago. Looking at the dry uncultivated country surrounding it is hard to believe that this was once considered prime sheep-raising country.

Much of the damage to the land has been caused by rabbits. Once the hills were alive with them and farmers resorted to desperate measures to try to control them. One farmer imported more than 200 cats from Christchurch and released them on his run. They didn't have much effect on the rabbits but they did on the birds. Stoats (toata) and weasels (tori uaroa), were also imported and these voracious killers spread with lightning speed along the length of the island with not much effect on the rabbits, although they undoubtedly contributed to the extinction of several bird species.

Other species had been wiped out before Pakeha arrived. Moa once roamed this area in vast numbers and one theory suggests that the forests were set alight to drive them into the open where they could be hunted. As well as the moa-hunter sites, moa feathers have been found buried in silt at Alexandra and in 1899 a gold dredge on the Clutha unearthed a perfect moa egg which earned the dredge hand the princely sum of £50 when it was bought by the Otago Museum in Dunedin. Throughout this area large finds of moa bones have been made, both in natural deposits such as swamps, where large numbers of birds were trapped, as well as in middens, where they were cooked for food. By all accounts moa lingered in the south considerably longer than elsewhere.

Other extinct birds were once found here. Finsch's duck, a flightless species, was first named from bones found in 1870 in the Earnscleugh Cave near Alexandra and a number of other extinct species, such as the eagle, goose, swan and pelican have been depicted in cave paintings throughout the region. It is thought that these were painted by moa hunters and travellers during the 14th and 15th centuries.

Around Alexandra ranges rise on all sides. To the north lie the broad reaches of the Dunstan Range and to the south and west the Old Man Range. This latter range is remarkable for being home to a number of native plants as well as for its many spectacular tors – impressive pillars of schist up to 15 m tall. This range is worth taking time to explore but be careful: Central Otago weather changes with treacherous suddenness even in summer and severe snowstorms can occur at nearly any time of the year.

From Alexandra SH85 runs north-east for some distance along the Manuherikia River before turning south-east through the gap between the North Rough Ridge and the Hawkdun Range towards Ranfurly and eventually the coast at Palmerston. At Waihemo, some 30 km before Palmerston, a side road leads south to Macraes Flat, considered remarkable by reptile researchers for the seven species of one genus of lizard, *Oligosoma* spp., that can be found living here in one small area – the only place in the world where this density occurs.

Palmerston is about 10 km south of Shag Point and this is worth using as a base to see the seabirds – although there are not, in fact, many shags. Cape pigeons are quite common along the coast together with giant petrels and sooty shearwaters and further out from shore large numbers of albatrosses and mollymawks can be seen.

Not far north of Shag Point is Moeraki where the famous round boulders are found on Koekohe Beach many weighing several tonnes and up to 2 m high, formed about 65 million years ago and protected in a scientific reserve. On the tiny island of Maukiekie, just offshore, there are little shags, spotted shags and our northernmost colony of Stewart Island shags. They all breed here along with one of the few colonies of royal spoonbills known to nest on an island.

If you have time, check out the area around Duntroon on SH83, about 40 km drive northwest of Oamaru. Here around Duntroon and the neighbouring settlement of Otakaieke are some of our best exotic trees. At the Campbell Park Estate, just outside Otakaieke, are a number of record-holding trees planted by the Hon. Robert Campbell around 1865. These include the world's largest coulter or big cone pine and some of New Zealand's largest giant redwoods and Douglas firs.

Turning back south, it is about 25 km to Waikouaiti where at nearby Island Point in the early 1840s the collector Percy Earl excavated a large number of moa bones. The naturalist Walter Mantell found more here in 1849 and made other collections further north at two points he dubbed Paramoa and Awamoa. Since then these two names have often been erroneously cited as examples of Maori usage of the word moa in place names.

From here it is a fairly short drive to Dunedin where a stop of a couple of days is well worthwhile. There is plenty to see in the surrounding countryside and the Otago Museum is worth visiting. Their bird collection includes some of the best mounted specimens I have seen – the laughing owl (whekau) being particularly impressive.

There are many parks and gardens throughout the city and in the many patches of light bush a good number of both native and exotic birds can be found. Dunedin was one of the earliest places where large-scale importation of exotic birds took place. In 1871 there was great excitement when Richard Bills, who made a living by importing birds for acclimatisation societies, arrived in Dunedin with 1,000 birds, a remarkably high number for that time considering the difficulties that shipping birds then posed.

Blackbirds, thrushes, skylarks, and a variety of finches were imported. Robins were also an early arrival but were not successful because the canny Mr Bills brought only cock birds, figuring that no one would pay good money for the drab females. Rosellas are here as well, descendants of a mixed flock of crimson and eastern rosellas released from a ship in Dunedin's harbour, Port Chalmers, in 1910, after they were refused entry. One of only two lots of cirl buntings to be brought in went to Dunedin (the other went to Wellington). These have survived with most of them being found in the limestone country around Oamaru but isolated populations are also found in arable areas along the east coast of the South Island, flocking together with Yellow Hammers in the non-breeding season. The cirl bunting, incidentally, is now one of the UK's rarest birds – perhaps we could send some back.

Another importation the society made which has earned it criticism is that of the little owl (koukou). This was first imported between 1906 and 1910 from Germany to control small birds which were attacking fruit. They succeeded only too well and the grubs which the birds had kept under control soon flourished. The owls also infuriated bird societies by attacking native species.

Two birds which have earned Dunedin justifiable fame are the yellow-eyed penguin (hoiho), and the royal albatross (toroa). At Taiaroa Head, not far from the city, is found the only mainland breeding colony of this beautiful albatross. It apparently tried to breed at this site for a number of years but was disturbed by animals and bird egg collectors. Then in 1937 Lance Richdale, a keen naturalist, took it upon himself to protect the bird, and the first chick was reared. Richdale is better known for his work with the yellow-eyed penguin, but it is almost certain that without his interest – which sometimes meant sitting all day beside the nest – the colony would not have become established. Now a small but growing colony of royal albatrosses is established at Taiaroa Head and thousands of visitors come each year to see the birds.

The yellow-eyed penguin is, on the other hand, in serious decline. Needing forested coastline near deep water to breed, the bird is under threat as this type of cover has been cleared for farming or by fire. Stock have also disturbed breeding birds and local Forest and Bird Society members have fenced off breeding areas but the Hoiho still needs all the help that it can get.

Opposite Taiaroa Head are the extensive salt marshes and sand flats of Aramoana, an important feeding ground for shorebirds as well as a breeding ground for fish. Large numbers of invertebrates and shellfish can be found here and the Aramoana cockles (pipi) are said to be the country's largest. Waterfowl also frequent the area and as many as 300 black swans (kakianau) have been noted. In the late 1970s, it was proposed that an aluminium smelter be built at Aramoana, but the scheme was shelved after massive opposition. The famous artist Ralph Hotere painted a series of protest artworks against the smelter. Aramoana later became a conservation area.

Leaving Dunedin take SH1 south to Balclutha and from there follow the Southern Scenic Route to the Catlins Forest. A wedge of undulating country running inland between the Clutha and Mataura rivers as far as the town of Gore, the Catlins is one of our least known wilderness regions and certainly deserves more attention than it currently gets.

Seals were once found along these southern shores in large numbers and although fur seals are the only ones now breeding here, it is probable that in the past other species did as well. The remains of large numbers of Hooker's sea lions together with numbers of sea elephants and sea leopards have been found in middens throughout the country. These, along with the remains of the occasional Weddell seal, crabeater seal and Ross seal, turn up on this southern coast from time to time.

That these animals had Maori names is significant as it indicates their regular occurrence on our coastline. Fur seals, *Arctocephalus forsteri,* are known variously as kekeno, or pakaka; the New Zealand Sea Lion formerly known as Hooker's Sea Lion as patoko or whakahao; the sea elephant as ihu koropuka; and the sea leopard was called popoiangore.

If the seal populations had survived the depredations by Maori, their very existence was threatened by the mass slaughter unleashed by the sealers who arrived in 1810. By 1840, when settlers arrived in the Catlins area, the seal colonies had been wiped out.

Also in 1840 the Sydney-based whaling captain Edward Cattlin arrived to assess the navigable possibilities of the river which now bears his name, though missing a 't'. For the equivalent of about $185 in cash and guns, Cattlin bought from local Maori the land stretching for 32 km on each side of the Catlins River and running 90 km inland. After years of negotiation that lasted 17 years after the captain's death most of this purchase was disallowed.

By the 1870s saw millers were hard at work and for about a century felling of the beech forests by up to 30 sawmills at one time continued unabated. When milling ceased very little tall timber was left and most of this was confined to reserves or inaccessible high areas.

Today Nugget Point is probably the best place from which to start exploring the Catlins. This long, narrow headland can be reached through Romahapa and by way of Kaka Point. From the end of the road take the path to the lighthouse from which far below the Nuggets can be seen, looking like the eroded fangs of some defunct taniwha. (Definitely not a place for anyone with vertigo!) On the rocks below can be seen a wealth of wildlife: fur seals haul out here and a number of seabirds, including red-billed gulls, gannets, spotted shags and white-fronted terns, breed in the locality.

At many places along the coast hoiho also breed so, if you should come across this bird, leave it alone. It is now our rarest penguin and any unnecessary disturbance can make it abandon its chick.

The first accessible beach in the Catlins is Cannibal Beach, named for bones found here by the early settlers. Nearby is the Catlins River and along its banks not far from the mouth is the Pounawea Reserve with some significant old trees.

Further along the coast is Jacks Bay with the island of Tuhawaiki just offshore. Large numbers of little blue penguins and sooty shearwaters breed on Tuhawaiki, using burrows dug in the clay cliffs and there are also some hoiho.

Heading inland through Ratanui and Tawanui brings you into the Catlins Forest Park. This area is thought to have been one of the last where moa survived and archaeological evidence of this has been found along the banks of the Tahakopa River which flows through the park a little further south. The park itself contains a number of birds, including tui, kaka, bellbirds, riflemen and a few yellowheads. Whio are also still found here and this is one of the very few places on the east coast of the South Island where it still occurs.

Continuing along Southern Scenic Route brings you to Papatowai, which is not far from Forest and Bird's Lenz Reserve at Tautuku, which it is hoped will eventually become an 'Ark in the Park' for the South Island. This project covers an area of 6,600 ha which includes a wide variety of habitats: lowland forests, wetlands, pingao sand dunes and manuka-dominated scrubland. This of course means that there is a wide range of fauna including long-tailed bats, kakariki, fernbird and rifleman. There are also several Galaxiids and the endemic Tautuku gecko, *Mokopirirakau cryptozoicus,* which is as its name denotes cryptic.

Continuing along the south coast brings you to the beautiful Tautuku Bay. The golden crescent of sand is separated from dense forest by a narrow strip of scrub and the contrast between sand and forest, all framed by a blue sky on a fine day, is glorious. Opposite the beach, about halfway along, is a track that leads to a beautiful pool in a splendid sylvan setting, rather grandly known as Lake Wilkie. Just across from the Lake Wilkie signpost can be found the Taurekei Forest Reserve. This is 550 ha of choice bush which has been preserved by the Forest and Bird Society and is well worth exploring.

Continuing on through Quarry Hills, Tokanui and Fortrose brings you at last out onto the extensive plains surrounding Invercargill, and only a short distance from the famed Awarua/Waituna wetlands, regarded as the most important in the country. Here, just a few metres from the southern ocean, grows one of the finest assemblages of alpine plants to be found, including cushion bog, creeping lily, comb-sedge, purple orchids and bladderworts. These are all plants you would normally expect to see high in the mountains, but it does not take long to find out why they are growing here. Stand still for a few minutes and you will catch a full blast of wind which feels as though it is straight off the polar ice cap.

Waituna is probably best known for its birdlife. In summer as many as 17 migratory wader species come here from the Northern Hemisphere and together with these are numerous residents. Considering that Waituna is about as far south as a migratory wader can get, the number of rarities which show up here is amazing.

Local ornithologists have seen in recent years Mongolian dotterels, grey plovers, sanderlings and Asiatic whimbrels – all rare visitors to New Zealand and seldom recorded elsewhere. In all, over 80 bird species have been recorded.

Behind the nearby town of Bluff there is a small forest-covered hill, which, now the possums and cats are being controlled is flourishing. Also flourishing in the forest are South Island robins (toutouwai) which were liberated here a few years ago after an absence of over a century.

Nearby Invercargill is more interesting than beautiful. It is known for its invigorating climate and the wide streets have been cunningly designed so that we less robust northerners can enjoy the wind to the full. There are numerous parks and gardens and in less bracing weather wandering among them is pleasant.

Invercargill is the centre of an extensive mixed farming area. In spring there are lambs in their thousands but these are subject to the vagaries of the Southland weather.

There are numerous rivers throughout Southland and these are popular with whitebaiters in the spring who catch these tiny fish as they make their way upstream. They are also popular with many birds which come from the north each year to breed. Masked lapwings, formerly called Spur-winged plovers, first appeared hereabouts on their arrival from Australia in 1932 and have since spread northwards throughout Aotearoa. Magpies are, on the other hand still spreading south and have now extended their range into Southland. They are aggressive and predatory birds and with luck Foveaux Strait/Te Ara a Kiwa will act as a barrier to their colonising Stewart Island.

Drive east from Invercargill and a drive of about an hour or so takes you back into beech forest. These trees are a delight to walk through for Northerners who are used to struggling through bush overgrown with scrub, lianas and vines. The light filtering down through the upper branches of the bosky beech forest provides an almost ethereal air – giving a particular grace and beauty to be experienced in few other types of forest.

There are about 40 species of beech in the Southern Hemisphere and New Zealand is home to five of these. These are the Hard Beech and Red Beech species, both of which also go by their Maori name Tawhairanui; the Silver Beech or Tawhai; and the Black Beech and Mountain Beech, both called Tawhairauriki.

Although there are some beech trees in the North Island they are nevertheless a South Island mountain tree coexisting with their own group of attendant species.

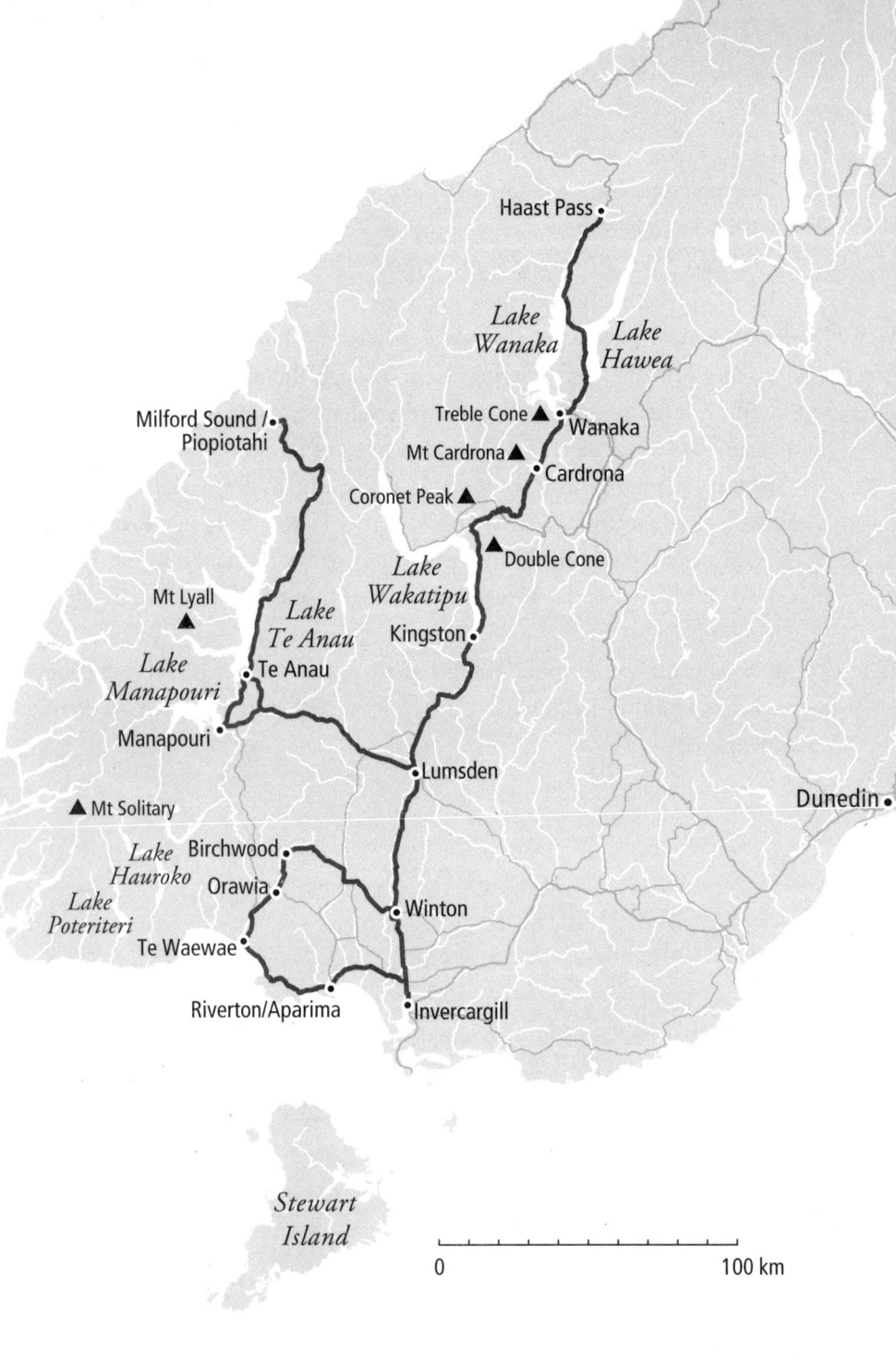

CHAPTER 14

Fiordland and Central Otago/Ata Whenua and Maniototo

From Invercargill north to Lumsden the road takes you through areas predominantly given over to mixed farming. Just past Winton on SH6 the road forks. The road to the left, SH96, arcs in a wide sweep towards the foothills of the Takitimu Mountains, past the old coal mining towns of Nightcaps and Ohai, then south again to Tuatapere, and eventually back to Invercargill via Riverton on SH99.

SH6, on the other hand, continues almost straight ahead, crossing the sheep and dry stock farming country on the western side of the Hokonui Hills, then across the Waimea Plains to Lumsden. A couple of kilometres past Lumsden turn left onto SH94 for Te Anau.

Just north of Mossburn, the first town past Lumsden, is a very large colony of black-billed gulls (tarapuka), a species once confined to the South Island. The colony has several thousand birds and in early summer is a hive of activity with dozens of birds returning with food for their squawking chicks. Since the late 1930s the tarapuka has been colonising the North Island, mostly in inland areas around lakes. It is regarded as the world's most endangered gull. In recent years these birds have often been unnecessarily harassed causing them to abandon their chicks. Masked lapwings breed in pairs within sight of the road, but don't go too close – they can be aggressive.

From Mossburn the road crosses a plain, passes over the Mararoa River and then climbs into the rain shadow area of the eastern foothills of the Alps to the once rabbit-infested plain called the Wilderness. The rabbits are no longer in their former numbers, but there are still many signs of the damage they inflicted. Areas of low-growing scrub and bog pine predominate with plenty of spinous piripiri, which does well in rabbit country.

From here the scenery changes dramatically as the road moves into the high mountains, but it is not until one arrives at the shore of Lake Manapouri that the full grandeur of the country becomes apparent.

Lake Manapouri is often described as our most beautiful lake however this claim has been made about many lakes in the South Island, but after travelling across the dry, dusty plains from the east, the effect of arriving suddenly on its shores is stunning.

Before you lies a vast expanse of silvered water with small, bush-clad islands scattered about like gems and beyond it all, as the perfect backdrop, the frieze of the Fiordland mountains. No matter how sunny the weather an air of moody, brooding beauty hangs over Manapouri, accentuated by the dark forested fringe running along the shores.

It is not only the scenery which draws people here. Manapouri is famous among anglers for the sizeable brown and rainbow trout and Chinook salmon caught here.

From Manapouri it is only a short drive to Te Anau township on the shores of the lake of the same name. Te Anau is the largest of the South Island lakes – 66 km long and with a shoreline of over 500 km. Its three long arms – the North, Middle and South fiords – push west from the main body of the lake deep into the Fiordland mountains.

In 1889 Australian Richard Henry, a naturalist and a conservationist well before his time, came to Te Anau tempted by a government offer of a £50 reward for an easy route to the West Coast. Travelling from the north-west arm of Middle Fiord he reached George Sound via what became known as the Henry Saddle.

Fascinated by the wildlife of the area, Henry stayed on and built a small hut on the shore. He acquired a five metre boat which he named the 'Putangi' after the Paradise shelduck and with this he explored the lakeshore and surrounding forests becoming an authority on Te Anau's birdlife.

When Henry arrived, birds abounded. Across the lake from his hut kakapo, piopio, tieke, kokako, little spotted and brown kiwi flourished. But as early as his first year Henry saw the signs of things to come. Cats and rats were beginning to infest the country and the first mustelids – stoats, weasels and ferrets – were seen, infiltrating at an alarming rate from the east, where the government had introduced them in a futile attempt to control rabbits. In 1883 Henry wrote:

> *Someone has put ferrets across the Waiau, under Mt Luxmore. I was trapping rabbits there and caught two ferrets, so I think the end of the kakapo has already begun.*

A few years after this in the nearby Hollyford Valley, the surveyor E. H. Wilmot noted that the kiwi, kakapo and weka had almost disappeared because of predation by mustelids.

It is all rather ironic that the takahe, the bird that was to be the object of much of Henry's efforts and attentions throughout his time in Fiordland, remained hidden away just over the ridge pottering around among the tussock in a hidden valley.

The discovery of the first takahe at Duck Cove, Resolution Island, in 1849 was reported by Dr Gideon Mantell at a meeting of the Zoological Society of London:

> *This bird was taken by some sealers who were pursuing their avocations in Dusky Bay. Perceiving the trail of a large and unknown bird on the snow with which the ground was then covered, they followed the footprints until they obtained a sight of the Notornis, which their dogs instantly pursued, and after a long chase caught alive in a gully of a sound behind Resolution Island. It ran with great speed, and upon being captured uttered loud screams, and fought and struggled violently; it was kept alive three or four days on the schooner and then killed and the body roasted and eaten by the crew, each partaking of the dainty which was declared to be delicious. The beak and legs were of a bright red colour. My son secured the skin.*

The second takahe was caught in 1851 on Secretary Island opposite Deas Cove in Thompson Sound, the third and fourth around Te Anau, near the

Mararoa River in 1879 and in the Middle Fiord in 1898 respectively, the latter bird being purchased from its finder, Donald Ross, for the then princely sum of £250 and preserved in the Otago Museum.

It was 50 years later, in 1948, that Dr Geoffrey Orbell, while on a hunting expedition, discovered a small number of takahe in a remote valley on the western shores of Lake Te Anau. Since then the Wildlife Service, now the Department of Conservation, DoC, has invested a great deal of effort in an attempt to breed takahe in captivity, first at Mt Bruce/Pukaka in the Wairarapa, and more recently at Burwood, near Te Anau, without much success initially. It is only when the idiosyncrasies of the takahe and its sex life were understood that captive breeding took off – so successfully, in fact, that a number of takahe have been released back into the Southern Alps.

They are also now established on a number of our off shore islands where as they are a very confiding and beautiful bird it is easy to see why they have become a firm favourite of visitors. Recently takahe have been released on the Gouland Downs and, as already mentioned, in the Kahurangi National Park.

The related North Island bird known by Maori as Moho or Mohoau, was still extant when Europeans arrived but seems to have vanished about the end of the 19th century.

To my mind, the takahe, the most beautiful of our native birds, deserves all the help it can get. Gerald Durrell describes his first meeting with a takahe in Takahe Valley:

> *There stood a bird the size of a large turkey – but more rotund in shape – and against the background of dark beech leaves and pale blonde snow grass, he glowed like a jewel. He had a heavy almost finch-like beak that, like his legs, was scarlet; his head and breast were a rich Mediterranean blue, and his back and wings a misty dragon green.*

Because of the lake and the flatlands to the east Te Anau is popular with a variety of birds. Upwards of 10,000 paradise shelducks winter in the Te Anau area. Occasionally the chestnut-breasted shelduck, a rare vagrant from Australia, has been seen here too, and one pair has nested and reared ducklings

at Glenmore Tarns near Lake Tekapo. Hopefully they'll prosper.

The name Te Anau is actually a corruption of the Maori name Te Ana au – rushing waters in a cave – but it was not until the 1940s that the caves were rediscovered across the lake from the township, at the base of the Murchison Mountains. It is a half-hour boat trip to get there but it is one well worth doing. Like the more famous Waitomo Caves in the North Island the caves have a glow-worm (titiwai) grotto and sport a glorious array of stalactites and stalagmites. In addition, there is an underwater waterfall. If you have the time and inclination, take a tramp inland to the upper entrance of the cave system. This is enormous – big enough to swallow a jumbo jet. Inside, a labyrinth of tunnels stretch off in all directions and in these a number of noteworthy fossils have been found, including the bones of the Stephens Island wren, formerly thought to be confined to that island, and those of a frog, four times larger than those native species existing today.

Today Te Anau town derives its income from two main sources – tourism and deer. Around the turn of the century four kinds of deer were released here – axis deer, moose, wapiti and red deer, with survival rates of nil, poor, moderate and phenomenal respectively. It is estimated that over one million red deer have been killed by both amateur and professional hunters since protection was removed, but they are still in sufficient numbers to cause concern by grazing vegetation and accelerating erosion.

From Te Anau to Milford Sound SH94 first takes you along the shores of the lake, then through the Eglinton Valley – tussocklands set among beech forest. Further on are the Mirror Lakes, with a superb view up Mistake Creek to Mt Ngatimamoe. This mountain was named for one of the South Island's earliest tribes, Kati Mamoe.

After the Mirror Lakes the road passes Cascade Creek and then Lake Gunn, a beautiful small lake set among bush and framed by the western mountains. The road then climbs the Divide and from there stretching northward is the Hollyford Valley, one of the most beautiful in New Zealand and the setting for one of Fiordland's justifiably famous walks.

From here the road then descends steeply to the west, offering tremendous views of the peaks and precipices of the upper Hollyford Valley, dominated by the 2,502 m peak of Mt Christina. It continues westward up the Upper Hollyford to the Homer Tunnel, emerging into the bush of the Cleddau Valley and then follows the river down to Milford Sound.

Milford Sound offers the best fiord scenery in the Southern Hemisphere, and there is not much in the Northern Hemisphere to rival it. A boat trip around the fiord will enable you to take in the best of the other natural features of Milford Sound: the snow-capped heights of Mt Pembroke; the Bowen Falls cascading from their high hanging valley; and the Lion dropping sheer-sided into the fiord depths. (The Lion's official name is Mount Kimberley.) Superb views of Mitre Peak can be had from the head of the fiord and fur seals are often to be spotted sun-basking on the rocks. Also found here are the little blue penguin and the Fiordland crested penguin whose colourful crown of yellow head-feathers, combined with bright reddish brown eyes, have earned it the sobriquet the 'punk-rocker' of the penguin world.

Running into Milford Sound is the Sinbad Valley which was home to the last kakapo to survive on the mainland. There are also a few lizard species which have so far only been found here but their habitat is sufficiently vertiginous that it deters poachers.

Piopiotahi in Milford Sound is the source of a soft, translucent stone known as tangiwai, which was prized, like greenstone, by Maori for use in ornaments and they journeyed here from considerable distances to gather it. The name Piopiotahi means 'one piopio', another reminder of our lost birds.

There are other points of note for the naturalist in Milford Sound. The silvereye, also known as the white-eye or wax-eye, was first noticed here in 1832, presumably not long after it arrived from Australia, and from here it began its northern spread. By 1856 it had become established in Canterbury and Nelson; by 1863 it had reached Whanganui; by 1865 it was observed in Auckland and then in the Bay of Islands in 1867.

Ten moose were liberated here after being imported from Canada in 1909. Their descendants, if still in Fiordland, are very low in number – probably no more than five animals scattered over some 400 sq. km. Only five are known to have been shot by hunters, the first in 1929 and the last in 1952. There are still a few optimists who think a few might survive, along with occasional reported sightings. Locals dub this 'the wild moose chase'.

Fiordland's spectacular sheer-sided sounds were gouged out of the mountains during the last ice age. The western heights are greatly affected by the winds of the Roaring Forties and rain falls in prodigious amounts – almost 7,300 mm a year on average at Milford Sound – making Fiordland one of the wettest places on earth.

This high precipitation nourishes the lush beech forest with its dense undergrowth. Higher up, nearer the treeline, this gives way to stunted beech, leatherwood and mountain fuchsia (kotukutuku), their branches festooned with hanging, delicate grey lichen called Old Man's Beard (hinakura).

Despite the rain, the steep-sided fiords offer good, sheltered anchorages which attracted sailors from the time of Cook onwards and made Fiordland, along with Marlborough and Northland, a site of much early scientific discovery.

Most of this work was centred in Dusky Sound, which although inaccessible by road can be reached by floatplane or by launch and by track from the Manapouri Hydro Scheme via the Spey and Seaforth rivers. Here at Dusky Sound James Cook spent nearly seven weeks in 1773 and during this time the ship's naturalist, Johann Rheinhold Forster, did a great deal of collecting. Of the 36 species collected here, some 30 were later described and have Dusky Sound as their type locality.

Sometimes, however, collecting seems to have been a bloody affair. After one foray Forster wrote: *At our return we found about nine shags, about 40 waterhens, 2 ducks, one curlew, one woodcook, one sandpiper, 11 large pigeon, several pohebirds [tui] two large parrots, a parakeet & several small birds had been killed.* Cook himself shot a whio – a *Duck of Blue Grey Plumage with the end of its bill as soft as the lips of any animal.* Birds were not the only animals collected. The crew landed fish at every opportunity and among those listed as caught were blue cod, scorpionfish, trumpeters, scarlet wrasse and tarakihi. The local wildlife must have been greatly relieved when they finally set sail.

After Cook, things were never the same again in Dusky Sound. By the end of the 18th century sealers had arrived and within a few years had annihilated the fur seal colonies. The first living takahe to come to the attention of the scientific world was collected here at Dusky Sound in 1849 and Richard Henry, mentioned earlier, started transferring endangered birds from here to island sanctuaries in 1895.

Henry was a naturalist of great talent, endless patience and with a boundless sympathy for his *strange wingless birds and flightless ones too*. Working often alone in primitive conditions, and in some of the worst weather imaginable, he transferred kakapo, great spotted kiwi and brown kiwi to Resolution Island in Dusky Sound. Kakapo were solitary creatures and each had an extensive home range of up to 50 ha, so capturing one meant a lot of hard work. During the period from April 1895 to December 1897, Henry moved a total of 474 kakapo and kiwi to Resolution Island, an average of 14 birds a month, a phenomenal achievement considering the primitive conditions under which he laboured. The fact that his efforts were unsuccessful in no way detracts from the magnitude of his work. As Don Merton wrote: *Had the sanctuary been a little further out from the mainland, out of swimming range of the stoats, the outcome may well have been different.*

An alternative route north from Lumsden takes you to Queenstown via SH6. The road passes through farmland much of the way but there are good patches of bush to be seen in the distance on the forested flanks of some of the ranges. The road goes first through Athol, past yet another Castle Hill, and then reaches Kingston on the southern shore of Lake Wakatipu.

Two of the islands, Pig and Pigeon, on Lake Wakatipu now have resident buff weka as does Mou Waho on Lake Wanaka, which were brought here from the Chathams/Rekohu in 2006 and 2008. These have settled in well and are breeding but chicks from these founding birds taken to the mainland have not prospered, due to the usual problems. To my mind the buff weka is a more attractively marked bird than that from the Stewart Island/Rakiura. Buff wekas were the eastern South Island race which became extinct on the mainland last century. Fortunately it had been introduced to the Chatham

Islands by settlers and is now there in good numbers. However, although it meant the weka was saved, it was disastrous for a number of the Chatham's already endangered species.

Lake Wakatipu is a Z-shaped lake more than 77 km long. Only Te Anau to the south and Lake Taupo in the North Island are larger. Despite its area its depth is surprisingly consistent.

Queenstown is 47 km from Kingston, at the head of Queen Bay where the lake takes a sharp turn westward. Situated at the foot of Ben Lomond, it is one of the prettiest of our towns and is nearly always thronged with tourists, well pre-Covid anyway. Queenstown deserves a leisurely exploration, so take your lunch and sit on the wharf and watch the enormous trout in the clear water. Along with these are scaup scooting along the lake floor with their distinctive swimming action and the rare black-billed gulls sitting on the wharf and foreshore, showing off their pristine white and grey feathers.

Although there is not much evidence of it today this area was once largely forested. Moa seem to have been quite common and several notable archaeological finds have been made. At Hawksburn, west of Alexandra, a 13th century midden containing the charred remains of nearly 700 moa were found, together with the typical stone blades and choppers of moa hunting sites. One of the best preserved moa remains comes from Queenstown – the dried head of a little bush moa, *Megalapteryx didinus,* which was found in a cave near the town.

For the tree fancier, the largest known conifer in New Zealand, a Californian big tree, grows in Queenstown, and at 37.7 m it is only half-grown. Particularly in autumn, the many exotics around the district are most attractive – a mass of glowing golds and reds. Also worth checking out is the very nice female Monkey Puzzle tree among the lovely trees in the Queenstown Gardens.

From Double Cone, the highest peak of the Remarkables, a few kilometres south-east of the town, extraordinary views can be had of mountains and vales stretching off in all directions. The most prominent are Pikiratahi/Mt Earnslaw and Tititea/Mt Aspiring to the north-west and, far to the north, Aoraki/Mt Cook.

A trip to Lake Hayes/Te whaka ata a Haki-te-kura, just out of Queenstown along SH6, is essential for any naturalist, even for the less energetic. Go in autumn when the exotic trees around the lake are in full colour. The sapphire waters of the lake behind the golden rim of poplars and willows and the rugged hills rising behind them are an unforgettable sight. The lake itself is a wildlife reserve noted for its waterfowl/puwhakawai. Large numbers of coots are now found here, together with scaup and pukeko and various other species. There is also good fishing with large brown trout and perch being caught.

Arrowtown, some 25 km north of Queenstown on the west bank of the Arrow River, dates from the heady days of 1862 when William Fox found gold here. It has some of the best restored colonial buildings in the country and is particularly charming in autumn when the autumnal colours are at their best. A very fine cedar of Lebanon grows at Thurlby Domain, about seven kilometres from Arrowtown. At almost 40 m tall, this tree has easily surpassed anything in its native Asia Minor where 25 m is considered to be a tall tree.

From Queenstown there are two routes north to Wanaka. The main route is SH6 which follows the banks of the Kawarau River to Cromwell, then on to Lowburn, Mt Pisa, Queensberry and Luggate. Colourful Californian poppies can be seen in many places, particularly where there are old mine tailings. Near Luggate, a spectacular series of terraces can be seen where the Clutha River has cut into the layers of gravel.

By comparison, the alternative route via the Crown Range and Cardrona Valley is more spectacular. Often covered in snow, in winter chains must be carried and the road is challenging for inexperienced drivers. Yet there are stunning views from the Crown Terrace, above the Arrow Basin, and again from the pass over the range, which at 1,121m is the highest main road in the country. From here the green waters of the Kawarau River can be seen snaking their way along their course far below.

Gold was discovered at Cardrona also but little remains there now to show for it. Further down the road, about 5.5 km from Wanaka, is a marvellous view of Mt Aspiring soaring to 3,036m in the north-east. Lake Wanaka and the adjoining Lake Hawea fill glaciated valleys and this can be clearly seen in the smoothed and rounded hills surrounding the lakes, contrasting with the sharper peaks above them.

In a hot summer it can be dry and bleak around Wanaka and in winter when the lakeside trees lose their leaves their skeletal forms bestow a drear and desolate aspect to this lake. But in spring, Wanaka is enchanting. Take the road from Wanaka to Glendhu Bay at this time and you can enjoy the trees that line the road. These are mainly exotics – willows, poplars, maples and limes – but there are also kowhai, all giving charm to the countryside. I unashamedly admit to being a tree devotee and I am always seeking out exceptional trees both native and exotic and for me the highlight of each year is autumn with its glorious colours – crimson and carmine and everything in between. It is as the American Romantic Poet, William Cullen Bryant so aptly put it: *Autumn, the year's last loveliest smile.*

Why exotic trees do so well in Aotearoa is a source of some interest to foreign visitors, but this is due to our equitable climate which has often resulted in these trees reaching sizes much bigger than anything found in their place of origin. Conifers, cedars and firs all do well and I have given a few of the best examples now growing here in God's own elsewhere in the text. This fecundity is however a double-edged sword and wind-born seedlings are now aggressively colonising large areas of the upland areas of both islands but particularly in the South Island. These seedlings result in trees called wilding pines. They are chiefly Douglas fir and various pines, particularly Radiata pine, *Pinus radiata*, Shore pine, *P. contorta*, Ponderosa pine, *P. ponderosa*, and Monterey cypress *P. macrocarpa* but also include species such as rowan, elder, silver birch and willows. Figures are a bit fuzzy but it is safe to assume that wilding pines now cover almost two million hectares in area and are costing millions of dollars to try to control.

From Wanaka SH6 to the West Coast takes you north along the shores of Lakes Hawea and Wanaka, then follows the course of the Makarora River before climbing to Haast Pass, the gateway to the coast.

Before Pakeha came the lower Makarora River flats were covered with a dense mixture of shrubs and forest. Timber milling started here in 1861 and the logs were rafted down the Makaroa River across the lake and on to the gold-mining towns of Cromwell and Clyde. Flax milling was also an important industry in this area.

CHAPTER 15

West Coast/Te Tai o Poutini

Haast Pass is reached after yet another Castle Hill. At 562 m, it is the lowest pass over the main divide. It was long used by Maori on their way to the West Coast to find greenstone but the first European to arrive here was a Scots goldminer, Charles Cameron, in January 1863, followed later that month by the geologist Julius von Haast.

For a century packhorses and cattle were driven to the West Coast over a formed track, but the building of a road did not begin until 1929. It was a further 31 years before Wanaka and Haast were finally connected by road and not until 1965 that the road finally reached Paringa on the coast, thus completing SH6. Because of the notorious West Coast weather, there are often slips and washouts, but the road is seldom closed for long and rarely blocked by snow.

Forest here is mainly silver beech, but there are also patches of kahikatea, rimu, miro and matai. The birds include kaka, kakariki, korimako and tui, along with both cuckoos in season, together with the smaller bush birds. In 1863 von Haast found it *alive with woodhen and many Kakapos,* but these have long since disappeared. Instead, along the streams whio are often to be found and kea pay close attention to unattended cars, especially near the top of the pass. Be warned.

On both sides of the valley above Haast Pass subalpine scrub extends upwards for the first 100 or so metres above the treeline, then gives way to alpine scrub and herbs. Such vegetation is deceptive. It is more variegated than one would initially presume, so if you have time examine it closely, as much for its beauty and variety as for its botanical interest. The mountain buttercup, sometimes called the large white-flowered buttercup, flourishes here together with speargrasses and mountain flax, the buttercup doing particularly well where sheltered by snow totara and hebes. Also on scree slopes and in rocky areas look out for the spectacular Haast's scree buttercup. The striking Penwiper plant has also been found here.

Rainfall is heavy and regular but the wettest point is further down the road at Roaring Billy on the Haast River. Here the mean annual rainfall is 5,840 mm and rain falls on average 182 days a year. Ten kilometres from the pass the Haast River plunges down into a gorge filled with huge schist boulders and 2 km past this are the Thunder Creek Falls, a 30 m cascade which can be reached by a 100 m walk through a glade of pretty beech trees. At Clarke Bluff the Haast River joins the mighty Landsborough River and combined they surge towards the sea across a riverbed as much as a kilometre wide in places. The road accompanies it for much of the way.

The land of the West Coast is made up of a narrow coastal strip jammed between the Tasman Sea and mountains which are incredibly steep, rising to a height of 3,450 m in just over 30 km. This flatland varies in width from about 20 km wide to a narrow strip of beach just metres wide where the mountains meet the sea. Twelve large rivers and dozens of small ones cross the plain, all swift, often rough, and always cold, fed by the glaciers and mountain watersheds.

Where there is flat land much of it has been cleared, often in a rather half-hearted fashion with burnt stumps, charred logs and much regenerating scrub to be seen. On this open land are found cattle, sheep and deer and some time ago someone imported water buffalo, claiming that the conditions on the coast should suit them. Well, they are water buffalo.

The area between Cook River and Big Bay in Fiordland contains the country's last kahikatea forests and most extensive wetlands and together these support large numbers of forest and wetland birds. There are also vast swamplands here with waterways meandering through them, as well as numerous lakes of picture-book perfection offering mirror-like reflections of the surrounding forests and mountains.

The forests, particularly at the higher reaches, are largely rata and beech and, in the swampy ground, kahikatea. These kahikatea forests were once spread over much of the country but today it is estimated that only two per cent remain and these are in South Westland.

Haast is the first settlement of any size that one reaches on the coast. The isolation and dense forest, poor soils and climate of this part of Westland did much to deter settlement. Gold mining, sawmilling and more recently sphagnum moss harvesting have all come and mostly gone, but it was the opening up of the road that put Haast on the map. Some 300,000 travellers normally come through here each year and tourism is one of its more important industries. This has however seen a drastic downturn since the arrival of Covid, and it is difficult to predict what the future will bring.

Recent archaeological work has revealed that a series of extensive settlements were once in South Westland. Jackson Bay/Okahu was once the centre of a major trading network in greenstone taken from the Red Hills further south along the Cascade River.

Greenstone was of major importance to early Maori, both for the manufacture of ornaments and weapons and also because of its value as a woodworking tool. The demand for greenstone would have grown in importance when pa began to be built because the detailed internal carvings could be made only with greenstone.

Far from being the 'mosquito-infested swamp' of popular imagination the West Coast is rich in natural resources and has much to offer the visitor. Among the places to visit around Haast alone are seal and penguin colonies, kahikatea swamp forest, sand dune forest and the many waterways lined by flax and kowhai. Each of these has its own unique combination of animals and plants.

Twenty kilometres south of Haast are the Waiatoto Swamps and these are particularly good for wetland birds. Bitterns are here in good numbers but are hard to see. However, their distinctive booming can be heard on most summer evenings. In the 1890s this was the last place the now extinct New Zealand bittern (kaoriki), *Ixobrychus novaezelandiae,* was found. A tour of the Waiatoto River is well worthwhile.

Kiwi in South Westland, as in so many other places, were until recently faring badly. At its nadir volunteers in the Jackson Bay-Haast area heard only two kiwi calls in 1,000 hours of listening and none at all at Okarito – both once kiwi strongholds. This compares with an area such as north-west Nelson where 10,000 calls were logged in 1,000 hours of listening.

The road north between Haast and Fox Glacier follows the beach for the first 20 km or so. Watch out for little blue penguins (korara) crossing the road towards their nesting burrows in the bush, especially in the evenings – they have abysmal road sense! At Knights Point these are joined by Fiordland crested penguins and a colony of these can be heard in the scrub near the shore, adequately protected in the middle of a clump of giant nettles. The thickly padded coat of the crested penguin makes it impervious to the vicious spikes of the nettle as well as to sandflies (namu). The usual etiquette applies – watch them quietly from a distance.

When last down here we stayed a night in some cabins not far from Lake Paringa and here I was more aware of the sounds of the night than in any other part of New Zealand. No sooner had the crickets stopped chirping than the bitterns started booming in the nearby swamp. This sound, too, faded away, to be replaced by the noise of countless whistling frogs from all directions, with the green tree frogs adding a deeper resonance from the ditches and swamp, and moreporks and kiwi calling continuously from the nearby bush.

From Paringa north to the glaciers the road runs through glorious country. There are headlands soaring over raging seas far below. There are lonely driftwood- and pebble-covered beaches and tiny gem-like bays where fur seals loaf the day away. And there are beautiful patches of forest everywhere with the trees swaying gently in the inshore breezes. Everywhere, too, there are tree ferns in abundance.

In the forest around Fox Glacier, a chorus of bush birds can be heard. Korimako are plentiful, there are Kea and you may be lucky enough to see a weka. The glacier itself is spectacular, perhaps even more so than the Franz Josef Glacier further north – a great 13 km mass of blue-green ice slowly inching its way towards the sea. Stand at the foot of the glacier and a solid wall of ice curves away above you.

Another no exit road runs out to the coast at Gillespies Beach from the Fox Glacier Headquarters and passes Lake Matheson. Together with Mitre Peak it is one of the most photographed spots in New Zealand. From the car park just off the road a boardwalk leads around the lake and from this rimu, kahikatea, koromoko and lancewood can be seen with a riotous assemblage of smaller trees and shrubs. Stop anywhere along the boardwalk and, especially in the early morning, you will hear tui and korimako. Fantails (piwakawaka), often the South Island black morph, follow the visitor, not so much for their company as for the bugs the visitors disturb.

Lake Matheson/Te Ara Kairaumati appears suddenly through a leafy curtain and the steps down to a moored raft will give you the best views of the lake. On a really calm day the lake and its reflections are so perfect that it is difficult to tell which way is up in a photograph.

From Lake Matheson there is a walk of a little over an hour to Lake Gault and, although Matheson is more picturesque, Lake Gault is richer in birdlife. The great crested grebe (puteketeke) can be seen here and in the surrounding bush kaka, riflemen and other birds are not uncommon. Also near Lake Gault a new colony is being started for the endangered rowi.

After Lake Matheson take the road down to Gillespie's Beach, site of an old gold-mining settlement. This beach is wild and covered with an amazing variety of driftwood. The beach itself is made up of bands of gravel decorated with white, quartz pebbles and patches of black sand with golden stripes. From the car park take the track along the beach to the north and this will bring you to the fur seal colony. From the beach there are terrific views of the Southern Alps and the glaciers.

Twenty-three kilometres farther north, the Franz Josef Glacier can no longer be seen from SH6, but on a dull day there is no mistaking its presence, as a pale light emanates from the deep valley through which it moves. To see it, visitors must follow the valley road, whereupon the glacier comes into sight with dramatic suddenness – a river of white and blue ice flowing down from the snowfields high above, between the Baird and Fritz Ranges.

The glacier feeds the swift and turbulent Waiho ('smoking water') River

– the Maori name comes from the vapour rising from its ice-cold surface. It carries pieces of ice with it on its headlong rush towards the sea. From the access road, a short walk will take you to Peter's Pool, a tarn left behind as the glacier retreated.

North of Franz Josef a drive of perhaps 20 minutes down a no exit road off SH6 takes you to Okarito, justifiably famed for the breeding colony of kotuku, or white heron, on the Waitangiroto River lagoon north of the Okarito lagoon. Although indications are that they were once more widespread, when Pakeha arrived they had already been reduced to one small colony breeding on the Waitangiroto and a demand for kotuku feathers for the millinery trade reduced them still further, from 25 pairs in 1871 to about 4 in 1940.

Since then, with rigorous protection, the recovery has been slow but steady and today there are c. 160 birds at Waitangiroto, about half of breeding age. Little shags and royal spoonbills (kotuku ngutupapa) also nest here and trips to see all of these birds can be arranged. Alternatively a few kotuku are often to be seen fishing around the Okarito Lagoon.

The kotuku arrive here in September, which coincides with the whitebait run in the nearby river and disperse throughout the country after breeding is completed, which is usually sometime in January.

Thomas Potts was one of the first Pakeha to visit the heronry and although never noted for the restraint of his writing he is even more effusive about the kotuku:

> *One gazes with delight on the flight of the kotuku, on the purity of its plumage, relieved by the spear-like bill and black feet, whilst the movement of its arched wings lends an impression of aerial softness, like the waving of a delicate feathery fan, such as some gentle spirit might employ to win to the forgetfulness of slumber the restless soul of some warrior chief.*

Near the white heron nesting site, and framed by flax and forest, Lake Rotokino is yet another beautiful lake in this part of the country. It has a good number of giant kokopu. These are the largest of our galaxiid fishes

and probably the most beautiful, with a pattern of golden stars on a velvety brown background. They are also now much reduced in numbers through habitat loss. Being nocturnal, of course, they are difficult to see. However, the Auckland Zoo has some good exhibits of this fish in their nocturnal house. Their young are a small component of the annual whitebait run which is made up of the fry of a number of different fish.

Also in the Okarito area is to be found a major development in the struggle to protect the kiwi – in this case the conservation of the rarest of our five kiwi species, the rowi.

This kiwi was the cause of considerable surprise to the ornithological community when in the 1990s it was realised that this bird was an undescribed species and consequently in 1994, it was given the scientific name, *Apteryx rowi*. Research following from this discovery revealed that while the rowi had once been one of the most widespread kiwi species, living in a large part of the South Island and a considerable part of the lower North Island, by the 1990s the population had declined to 165 aging adults in the Okarito area. Rowi are a long-lived species; it is estimated that some birds live up to around 100 years of age, but the breeding rate of one chick per year was not enough to cope with the high rate of predation, chiefly by stoats.

Desperate measures were needed and implemented. ONE (Operation Nest Egg) started removing eggs from nests and these were incubated at the West Coast Wildlife Centre at Franz Josef township, the resulting chicks being removed to a kiwi creche where they remained until they were big enough to fend off predators when they were returned to Okarito.

One of the results of the dramatic recovery of the rowi is that the Okarito Sanctuary is now full, so a new sanctuary was started at Omoeroa near Lake Mathieson with the first group of chicks being released in 2018. A number of other rowi chicks are being used to start populations on offshore islands.

The Wildlife Centre is also working with another endangered kiwi, the Haast Tokoeka. This bird has now only a few hundred birds surviving in the wild, so the Centre is using the same methods as those used for the rowi, with resulting tokoeka chicks being returned to the wild at Haast. Visits can be made to the centre so check with the West Coast Wildlife Centre for details.

Okarito is the country's largest unmodified wetland and supports a wide selection of waterfowl apart from the kotuku and spoonbill and it is well worth spending a bit of time exploring.

Abut Head at the mouth of the Whataroa River is considered to be one of the most spectacular coastal landforms along the entire West Coast. It has long been rendered relatively inaccessible to development by rivers, lagoons and the sea, and this has also meant that it is still close to its original state with some of the best birdlife on the coast being found here.

Further up SH6, about 15 km north of Harihari is yet another of the West Coast's beautiful lakes. Byron's poem 'Childe Harold's Pilgrimage' was dedicated to Ianthe and the explorer who found this lake decided it would make a charming name for a charming lake. Ianthe covers an area of some 900 ha and is surrounded by kahikatea and matai forest.

One matai close to the road is reputed to be the largest in New Zealand. It is an enormous tree estimated to be over 1,000 years old. Ianthe supports good numbers of brown and rainbow trout and the birdlife too is prolific. More great crested grebes are found here than on any other Westland lake and scaup, shoveler and grey duck are also here in good numbers.

From Lake Ianthe the road north to Hokitika and Greymouth shows the actions of humans at their worst, against what was once some of nature at its best. Here and there farms have been cleared with much effort from the forest and the swamp, first by the pioneer with his firestick, spade and axe and more recently by his successors with chainsaw and bulldozer. Much work was needed to subjugate the forest and constant vigilance is needed now to keep it at bay. The forest crowds in from all sides, scattering its seed across the stolen acres and bracken and scrub spring up wherever the land is left unattended.

In this area gold mining has devastated much of the land. Once-fertile river flats worked over by gold dredges are now piled high with vast heaps of useless boulders and tailings. The land here lies stripped and ruined. Decades have done little to disguise the scars of their handiwork and centuries will do little more. Nothing much remains now of the colour of the gold rush except in old ghost towns such as Notown, Deadman's Flat, Candlelight and Nil Desperandum.

In the many areas where there are no farms or old goldfields, the bush stretches up from the lowlands to the hills in a green carpet and seems as untouched and untrammelled as when the tangata whenua first arrived. This is not so. Dead rata and other trees such as kamahi can be seen clearly from any vantage point – victims of possums. Pigs, deer and goats also wander unchecked over vast areas destroying saplings and regenerating undergrowth. The forests that once rang with birdsong are now too often silent, the birds having fallen victim to cats, rats and stoats and one is only too aware that even with the best will in the world and even with unremitting effort and limitless finances nothing can ever again be as it once was.

It is as William Pember Reeves wrote in 'The Passing of the Forest':

Gone are the forest birds, arboreal things,
Eaters of honey, honey-sweet of song,
The tui and the bell-bird – he who sings
That brief, rich music we would fain prolong,
Gone the wood-pigeon's sudden whirr of wings;
The daring robin, all unused to wrong.
Wild, harmless, hamadryad creatures, they
Lived with their trees, and died, and passed away.

Rivers between the Hokitika River and Greymouth were particularly prized for the greenstone that they yielded. The Taramakau River had in pre-Pakeha days a jade-working site near the river mouth. It produced large quantities including some of the prized kawakawa and inanga varieties and many artifacts have turned up here as a by-product of dredging operations.

The Arahura field produced a paler jade, and the strong green kawakawa variety preferred by Maori is not so often found here. However, many hundreds of tonnes of the various types have been mined over the years.

The early prospectors who came to this area were a more pragmatic lot than the pioneers of Canterbury and Nelson and had less time for the fripperies and bibelots of civilisation such as hunting and gardening, so fine old exotic trees such as those that grace many parts of the east coast are mostly absent here.

Instead, many of the exotic trees to be seen here date from 1932 when the steamer *Abel Tasman*, carrying a consignment of trees from New Plymouth to Australia, was wrecked at the mouth of the Grey River. Large numbers of trees were sold to the locals at one shilling each. One exotic tree that does date from much earlier, probably from the days of the gold rush, is a common lime just outside of Arahura, which is regarded by tree fanciers as the best example in the Southern Hemisphere.

Because the West Coast was forested for much longer than many other areas, it attracted the attentions of the early bird collectors, who sometimes took birds in large numbers. Of one collector on the Coast, Thomas Potts commented:

> *You are not expected to speak out on this subject of bird slaughter; you are numbered with the Philistines if you murmur at the wounding and maiming in the interests of museums; mortal offence was said to have been given by an indiscreet individual who recorded the fact that one collector alone killed and disposed of above two thousand specimens of the harmless kiwi.*

It is as a result of collectors such as these that kiwi are so common in museum collections worldwide. The first exhibit I saw in the Natural History Museum in Montevideo in Uruguay was a kiwi far from home.

Because the West Coast faces Australia more rare birds have arrived here than in any other part of the country, and recent arrivals include the Nankeen night heron, Australian darter, glossy ibis, and the Australian barn owl.

Butterflies, too, arrive on the West Coast, some annually. The blue moon, one of the most striking species, turns up each year as does the Australian painted lady and the Australian blue tiger. What is amazing is that so many of these delicate creatures survive the rigours of a stormy Tasman Sea crossing. However, the area does have butterflies of its own. The forest ringlet, *Dodonia helmsii*, one of the most attractive but least known endemics, was first discovered in its forests in 1881.

With a population of around 9,000, Greymouth is the largest town on the West Coast. It has much of interest to the naturalist. Hector's dolphin occur offshore along with a large variety of seabirds and by using Greymouth as a base much can be seen in the surrounding countryside. If you are interested in procellariid seabirds or dolphins a sea trip is recommended, but the river bar crossing can be invigorating.

From Greymouth there are two routes north. The first is inland along State Highways 7 and 69 to Inangahua Junction and from there either north to Nelson or back to the coast by way of SH6. The alternative route is the coastal road to Westport along SH6.

For those with an interest in history the inland route is recommended as it takes in many of the sites of the Coast's once frenetic gold mining activity. Here, the land was devastated by mines whose wealth, as the explorer Charles Douglas cynically observed, *goes directly home to the shareholders who never saw the land and who never intend to*. The forest is now gradually covering the scars of the worst excesses of this endeavour but it will be many generations before the land is completely healed.

Reefton, 79 km inland from Greymouth, is one of the few surviving mining towns, although with a population of under 1,000 is now a mere shadow of its former self. It does, however, provide access to the Victoria Forest Park. At almost 210,000 ha, this is one of our largest forest parks and despite some logging still has good stands of beech and mixed beech and podocarp forest. It also has the great spotted kiwi (roroa), brown kiwi, weka, kaka and whio along with such introduced species as red and fallow deer, pigs and chamois.

Some yellowheads are also still found here and it was near here that the naturalist William Walter Smith observed them moving through the bush in company with saddlebacks:

> On reaching near the top of the gully, I heard the shrill ringing notes of a flock of yellowheads... They numbered about two hundred, and were in rich plumage... before the yellowheads had quite disappeared I heard the

rich flute-notes of a flock of saddlebacks advancing... probably no scene in bird life is more attractive or beautiful...

For the naturalist, though, the coastal route offers more. The Point Elizabeth Walkway 11 km north of Greytown offers a walk through typical coastal vegetation whose 'shaven' appearance is due to the prevailing salt-laden winds. Also of interest, are the limestone bluffs that have been pushed by uplift to an impressive 300 m above sea level.

In the hills behind Barrytown, 34 km from Greymouth, nests one of the world's rarest seabirds, the Westland black petrel (taiko). This bird, once called the Westland shoemaker because of its distinctive call, survives only here in perilously low numbers but the sooty shearwater which once also nested here has now vanished. Yet in the hilly Paparoa Range, as well as in the Papahoe or Twelve Apostles Ranges, which lie inland from the road, there are still birds to be seen and heard and there is a wide range of vegetation of interest to the botanist. The great spotted kiwi is found here in moderate numbers but the other two kiwi species seem to have vanished.

It seems to have been the great spotted kiwi to which Charles Douglas referred when he wryly noted:

> *I have very little to say regarding this bird, as I have only seen two of them, and being pushed with hunger, I ate the pair of them: under the circumstances I would have eaten the last of the Dodos.*
>
> *It is all very well science lifting up its hands in horror at what I once heard called gluttony, but let science tramp through the Westland bush and swamps, for two or three days without food, and find out what hunger is. Besides, at the time, which was many years ago, I was not aware that it was an almost extinct bird. Had I known so I would have at least skinned it and kept the head and feet.*

Judging by the number of roadside casualties, this would seem to be a prime possum habitat. Harrier hawks find these easy pickings much to their liking and can often be seen flapping unhurriedly away at the approach of vehicle.

The Punakaiki or Pancake Rocks 15 km farther on from Barrytown are a popular tourist destination. Strangely sculpted columns of limestone rocks, they trap the incoming surf and funnel it upwards in explosive and spectacular bursts. Seal Island, some 7.5 km distance along SH6, although probably named for its shape, has resident fur seals and these can be seen from the signposted track running from the beach.

With a population of about 4,400, Westport is the Coast's second biggest town. If you are stopping over in the town, or just have time to spare, take a drive out to Cape Foulwind Lighthouse with its spectacular sea cliffs. It is about ten kilometres west of the town by way of Carters Beach.

Five kilometres further on is Tauranga Bay with its breeding fur seal colony, the pups from which can sometimes be encountered on the beach. Look but don't touch! Their mothers bite. The best way to get an overall view of the seal colony is to take the Cape Foulwind Walkway which offers several good vantage spots.

From Westport either turn inland and travel on to Nelson via Inangahua, named for and once famed for its whitebait, or continue north along SH67 to Karamea, a relatively easy drive of 98 km.

The Karamea road offers a variety of scenery, ranging from forested ranges to broad surf-swept beaches, but the flax, nikau palms and cabbage trees growing almost along its entire length give it a sort of visual unity. Apart from the climb over the Karamea Bluff it hugs sea level throughout the entire distance along the coastal strip jammed between mountains and sea. It also runs through what is, along with Fiordland and the Urewera country, some of the remotest and least populated land in New Zealand. This remoteness and emptiness has, however, had its compensations, preserving the scenic beauty of the region from the sometimes questionable development that has been the bane of other areas closer to populated centres.

'Winterless' Karamea benefits from a warm microclimate which gives the area some of the West Coast's best climate and supports a flourishing dairying industry along with some horticulture. Although much has been made of building a connecting road to Nelson this has so far come to nought, so to get there you must either walk by way of the Heaphy or Wangapeka tracks or take the road back south to Westport, then north west through Inangahua Junction. If the prospect of a 5 day walk doesn't exactly fill you with rapture, at least consider tackling the 15 km coastal section at the south end of the Heaphy Track, which is just up the coast from Karamea, at the Kohaihai River.

The highlight of the Karamea area is undoubtedly the Oparara Valley. Here there is a spectacular assemblage of caves, canyons and arches carved from the natural limestone and backed by granite ranges. At Honeycomb Hill, in a 13 km labyrinth of caves, one of the most important assemblages of bird fossils has been found. These caves and crevices acted over thousands of years as a huge trap for hapless birds which fell through potholes and also for the carcasses of those swept in by streams. So far the bones of some 52 species have been identified, of which 26 are those of species now extinct. Also identified from the caves have been the remains of lizards, frogs and land snails.

Living creatures also occur in the caves, the most imposing of which is probably the gradungular spider with a span of some 13 cm which preys on cave weta. There are also native fish such as the kokopu and the koaru, now rare elsewhere, to be found in the streams of the Oparara Valley.

Public access to the 'Honeycomb Hill Specially Protected Area' is restricted to DoC approved guided tours, due to the delicate ecological nature of the area.

And nearby also is one of the highlights of New Zealand's natural world. Nikau palms have their southern limit not far south of Karamea, making these the most southerly palms in the world. The meeting of the 'Ps' at this point – pigeons, parrots, palms, penguins and even possibly possums – make for a fascinating mixture of subtropical and sub-Antarctic, indigenous and exotic elements that is uniquely New Zealand.

CHAPTER 16

Stewart Island/Rakiura

If I had to nominate my favourite place in New Zealand I think it would have to be Stewart Island or Rakiura. Groups of little cottages charmingly set around tidy bays with clear waters, extensive stands of bush within easy walking distance of the settlement and a wealth of natural life all contribute to its appeal. Even the often lousy weather has its compensations. In the early morning it is a delight to see the mist creeping into Halfmoon Bay, softening the outlines of the offshore stacks and giving them a surreal quality.

When I first flew into the island from Invercargill I must admit to a little disappointment because from the air it seemed considerably smaller than I had imagined. Yet appearances are deceptive; Stewart Island is, after all, our third-largest island.

The island is roughly triangular in shape, with the west coast from Black Rock Point in the north to South West Cape being 60 km long. The entire length of this coast is exposed to the Tasman Sea and rollers thunder constantly onto the shore. The south-east coast is just as rugged and exposed but has the advantage of several good harbours and to these the first whalers and sealers came. Maori had called the island Rakiura – 'Island of the Glowing Skies' – but never seem to have settled here in any large numbers preferring Ruapuke Island, a short distance to the north-east.

On the east coast Paterson Inlet penetrates inland almost half the width of the island and running still further inland from the head of the inlet is the Freshwater River. This drains a large swamp which extends almost all of the way to the west coast, effectively dividing Stewart Island into two large, dissected massifs. This swamp is a favourite of waterbirds and fairly large numbers of these are to be found, including black swans and grey ducks. Brown teal were once also found here until fairly recently but have now vanished.

Stewart Island is one of the few places where the dawn choruses of early New Zealand can still be heard, probably because their songs are not drowned out by background traffic. Tui and korimako flock into the fuchsias which surround Halfmoon Bay and each morning there were at least a couple of dozen around the caravan park where we were staying. As these tui are nowhere near as timid as their northern cousins you can quite easily get close enough to hear the soft contemplative notes and trills which have been called their 'whisper songs'. The kereru or wood pigeon is also very tame, peering at you with the rather endearing, dim-witted air that only pigeons can affect.

Kaka are common here and are often heard as they fly high overhead. When I was last on Stewart Island the splendid gum trees on the road to Ackers Point were fruiting and the kaka were feeding on the gum nuts. These ferment with predictable results and after a few days the kaka were definitely the worse for wear. One dawn chorus that soon loses its appeal is that of a group of drunken kaka carousing atop your caravan for the third morning in a row. I watched one bird fly determinedly out of the gums and across the bay straight into a telephone pole. He slid down, shook himself, then flew off in considerably shakier fashion.

Larger birds are also found on Stewart Island. The brown kiwi or tokoeka is relatively common away from the settlement and can often be seen out and about in the late afternoon because the long days of summer allow insufficient time for birds to forage exclusively at night. They turn up in the main settlement, Oban, from time to time. If you meet up with one stand quietly and they will probably inspect your boots and then wander off. If you are tramping on the island look out for them among the flax and scrub, particularly around Mason Bay on the West Coast. We found numerous tracks on the sand there and spotted two kiwi about mid-afternoon.

The Stewart Island brown kiwi is larger than the two other sub-species of tokoeka found in the south and south-west of the South Island and it is now believed that the first kiwi to be collected and described was probably a local bird taken to Sydney by returning sealers. The type locality for this bird was subsequently given as the North Island which caused considerable confusion in later years.

Weka are here too and this is a different race than that to be found in the South Island. It has declined dramatically in recent years which is a great pity because, despite its kleptomania and other minor peccadillos, it is a charming character. Wekas were once considered to be a pest for their habit of stealing eggs from poultry runs and digging up gardens but in recent years none have been seen close to the settlement on Stewart Island. Ulva Island, in the middle of Paterson Inlet, is the closest point to Halfmoon Bay where they can now be seen. If you take your lunch with you to Ulva this practically guarantees a weka will drop by in the hope of a snack.

On Ulva, the larger trees have never been cut and rimu, totara, miro, kamahi and southern rata are all here in good numbers. Take one of the several excellent trails marked out through the island and from these, besides the larger shrubs and tree ferns many smaller plants, in particular, ferns and orchids, can be seen. In spring the Bamboo orchids and Lady Slipper orchids are very pretty. Besides weka there are the usual Rakiura bush birds but a number of others have been introduced. Probably the most interesting of these are South Island saddleback, riflemen, yellowheads and Stewart Island robins. It is interesting to consider that yellowheads (mohua) elsewhere are canopy dwellers in beech forest, but here on Ulva they adapted quickly to living at mid-levels in podocarp trees and can sometimes even can be seen foraging on the ground.

Stewart Island is, however, probably best known for its muttonbirds. Walk out to Ackers Point in the summer evenings and the dozens of muttonbirds landing around you will give you a faint idea of what it must be like on the islands offshore, where the birds are in their tens of thousands. The 350 ha of the Snares Group to the south of Stewart Island is home to an estimated 8 million muttonbirds and many of the smaller islands off Stewart Island once had correspondingly dense populations. When birds in these numbers are landing the din must be indescribable. Guthrie-Smith has left us a delightful description of this:

I turned in, and for a long time lay ruminating over the marvels of the evening flight, and listening to the night crammed with sound; at last, with the wail of innumerable petrels in my ears, I fell asleep to wake again at earliest dawn... Something had stopped, it was the sound of silence again returned that had roused me. The growing light had drawn the petrels down their flapped and wing-beaten paths; to the very edge of the cliffs had flowed their fluttering streams, runnels like those that never reach the earth, spilling themselves from the mountain heights of our southern sounds. The dawn had called like God; at its bidding each tenant had stepped from his dark tomb. It was the morning of the Resurrection. No wood birds sang, a silence had fallen on the earth blank as that of an extinguished star. In the chill of the morn and after the night of eager courtship a desolation brooded over the empty land, as when the Lord shall have called all living creatures to their last account, when wealth of leaf in spring and weight of autumn grain shall no more be known to the generations of man.

Who could ever call them muttonbirds again after reading this!

For the record the Maori name for the most common muttonbird, the sooty shearwater, is hakoakoa and titi is the name for the chicks when they are being harvested. Many other seabirds can also be seen around the island. Spotted shags, little shags and Foveaux shags are all found here together with the blue shag which goes under the rather unusual local name of the bravo duck. They mostly nest on the smaller islands and stacks offshore and their nesting places are clearly visible under the white coating of guano which has usually killed all vegetation in the immediate vicinity.

'Bravo duck' is not the only unusual local name I heard down here. Giant petrels are called stinkpots; kaka are often referred to as 'kaki' and a Scotsman I met called the giant petrels 'dirty Allans'. Best of all a friend always called the local albatross the 'wondering albatross' which conjured up pleasant pictures of the bird sitting on its nest looking pensive and perplexed.

Usually there are other seabirds, often gulls, nesting in association with the shags, even though their raucous calls and habit of regurgitating semi-digested fish makes them not particularly desirable neighbours. I borrowed a boat and spent a most enjoyable afternoon watching the comings and goings at a pied shag rookery, or shaggery as they are sometimes called. As each parent arrived, its chick would make an appalling din, wailing peevishly until the adult opened its beak. The chick thereupon plunged its head down the parent bird's throat for the fish inside and upon finishing it sat there crying piteously for more.

Penguins abound here, and on virtually any boat trip you will see little blue penguins diving as the boat approaches and then surfacing again some distance away. Fiordland crested penguins are here too with a few yellow-eyed penguins, but unlike the little blue most of these nest on the smaller offshore islands.

As settlement has increased around Halfmoon Bay, the little blues that once nested here have moved to less frequented areas. A number nest at Dead Man's Beach and I made several trips there to watch them wandering nonchalantly out of the tide in the evening. On the return trip to Halfmoon Bay, bats were always to be seen, a rare sight in the north, and moreporks were calling everywhere, their calls mingling with those of the seabirds passing overhead.

On my first trip to Rakiura I was fortunate in being able to make a couple of day trips out of Halfmoon Bay with local fisherman and enthusiastic birder Pete Tait and so was able to see a number of seabirds which normally keep some distance offshore. As soon as we cleared Ackers Point a line of red-billed gulls (tarapunga) alighted on the stern of the boat with all the self-assured aplomb of regular travellers and remained with us for most of the day. Although among the most common of our seabirds they are also among the most attractive, with their neat grey and white attire nicely set off by scarlet beaks and feet. Black-billed gulls don't seem to occur on Rakiura.

Further out near the crayfish pots, we picked up a number of other hangers-on. These included several shearwaters, Cape pigeons/Ttitore (sometimes known irreverently as Jesus Christ birds for their habit of pattering across the surface of the water), together with several species of mollymawks. These are spectacular birds, not as large as an albatross, but with their large wingspan dramatic all the same. With scarcely a wing beat they glide effortlessly in the wake of the boat but rapidly abandon all dignity when food is thrown their way. Although most of the species look similar from a distance, examination of their beaks and heads through binoculars enables them to be distinguished and from among those following us we identified the black-browed, Buller's and the shy mollymawk. (NB: In the North it is storm petrels which are known as Jesus Christ Birds or Jesus Birds.)

Fur seals are common outside Halfmoon Bay and are often to be seen sunbathing on the rocks fringing the various points and islands. When boats draw near they usually dive into the water, although they are not always so timid. Females with pups can get very aggressive when they think their young are threatened and a couple of the paua divers around Stewart Island have received nasty bites. After almost being exterminated in the sealing days, the seals are again on the increase and the staff at the salmon farms on the island are now complaining that the nets around their ponds have been ripped by seals trying to get at the fish inside.

Dolphins kept the boat company at several times during the trip, skipping along by the bow wave. These were either dusky or common dolphins, the most common species around here. Hector's dolphin is seldom seen off Halfmoon Bay but is often found between Stewart and the South Island. Even rarer is the beautiful hourglass dolphin which seems to have its range to the south of the island.

In the south of the island, in an area closed to ordinary visitors, a number of fascinating finds have been made, including the harlequin gecko *Tukituki rakiurae* our rarest and probably our most attractive lizard which has previously been illegally targeted by collectors. It is probably the world's most southerly lizard.

Also in the south, about 40 years ago, a colony of the very rare kakapo was found in a mountainous area called the Tin Range. The discovery was particularly exciting as the colony included females. The female kakapo is smaller than the male and more vulnerable to predators while sitting on its nest. As a result, all female kakapo had long since disappeared from elsewhere in the country, leaving only a few old bachelors.

Although free of mustelids, Stewart Island has feral cats which were taking the birds. With considerable effort, Don Merton, a renowned conservation officer who specialised in endangered birds, and other Department of Conservation officers, trapped a number of birds and these were sent north to Little Barrier Island in the Hauraki Gulf, one of our few predator-free islands. This must have been a dramatic change in climate for the kakapo, coming from the frozen wind-swept heights of the Tin Range to a subtropical island. Unfortunately, although the birds survived, no breeding took place. At the same time cat predation started to increase drastically in the Tin Range with a consequent sharp decline in the population and it thus became imperative to find somewhere else for the few remaining birds.

Codfish Island/Whenua Hou off Rakiura was selected. The major problem with Codfish was that it had a large weka population which had been introduced to the island by the early sealers. Weka are extremely efficient and determined hunters and in areas where they have been liberated they have decimated ground-nesting birds. Codfish is one of the few islands with nesting populations of Cook's petrel, or titi, and so far, the only place the rare whenua hou diving petrel has been found. Over the years weka had reduced both to very low numbers. For both birds' sake, as well as to help the kakapo's chances of breeding on Codfish Island, the weka were removed and many were released on Stewart Island. It is hoped that Codfish Island along with Hauturu and Anchor Island in Fiordland are launching points which will eventually mean that the kakapo can be reintroduced to the mainland.

Another bird which seems to have survived on Stewart Island after disappearing elsewhere is the South Island kokako. This was once regarded as a member of the crow family – although any resemblance to this formally attired bird is superficial – and one of the bird's early English names was the orange-wattled crow. Fortunately, its more attractive Maori name is now generally used. Although common on Stewart Island in the days of early Pakeha settlement they dwindled quickly in numbers and by the turn of the century were already rare. Herbert Guthrie-Smith travelled to Mason Bay, Port Pegasus and the Rakeahua River in 1910 to try to photograph this bird and although he saw one or two he was not able to record them on film. Despite this, his private notes on the habits of the bird are valuable:

> *Noticed a pair of crows feeding in the stinkwood eating their simple fare very delicately and like an epicure. When alarmed or startled or less than that, [they] make a line to their headquarters hopping on the ground with the confidence of often travelled tracks. They do not hop but each bough lends them its springing life, poetry of motion.*

'Poetry of motion' it may well have been, but this habit of moving on the ground would have served it poorly once cats arrived.

Rhys Buckingham, a Nelson ornithologist, was confident that there was an isolated population of kokako in the south around Port Pegasus. He heard calls there and a feather has been found further north in the Rakeahua Valley, so it seems that maybe the bird still survives, although perilously close to extinction. The South Island kokako differs from its North Island cousin by being a much more retiring bird, and as it does not spend its mornings calling from the topmost branches of trees, it is much more difficult to find. Probably the brisk winds of the south of Stewart Island play a part in this. Any bird which attempted a dawn chorus from the top of a tree would probably find itself whisked towards the Antarctic in very short order.

In a rather strange experiment, a few years back, a North Island kokako, who was a notorious misogynist, was taken to Rakiura to see if his calls could entice the locals. It didn't work.

Besides birds, Stewart Island also supports a great variety of plant life. The muttonbird scrub, with its large leathery leaves, seems to fill the role here of the pohutukawa further north. These leaves were once used as a novel way of sending postcards from the island, although the Post Office, rather unsportingly I feel, no longer allows this to be done.

Botanists say that every type of vegetation on the island differs significantly from that on the neighbouring South Island, developing its own individual forms during the 10,000 years or so of isolation. Many of these plants have been collected together and can be seen at the lovely Moturau Moana Reserve a short distance out of Halfmoon Bay on the road to Horseshoe Bay. The ferns and particularly the Prince of Wales feathers (heruheru) are especially attractive.

Out from Halfmoon Bay there are numerous walks which even the only moderately fit can tackle. For someone like me who fancies ferns, the clumps of crown and shield ferns are particularly good along the track following the old logging road towards Dynamite Point, but these ferns are unfortunately showing some of the effects of browsing by white-tailed deer. Another walk is the track which takes you north along the coast to Maori Beach. Look out for the tree ferns, in particular the mamaku, wheki-ponga and soft tree fern (katote) which do especially well in the more sheltered gullies where they are protected from herbivores. This enables you to see some of the finest coastal and bush scenery on the island and can reasonably be done in one day, so will get you back into the settlement in time for a drink.

Finally, seals (pakaka) and sea lions (kekeno) often haul out on the beaches for a snooze and most decidedly do not want to be included in your 'selfies'.

If you are not in the mood for brisk constitutionals and prefer peregrinations, or to just sit and think, or maybe just sit, there are few better places to do so than on Stewart Island. Pick a secluded bay or one of the many beautiful bosky glades of trees and experience some of nature at its best.